What if you defenses fail?

CYBER BREACH

Designing an exercise to map a ready strategy

REGINA PHELPS

Chandi Media

www.ChandiMedia.com

260 Whitney Street
San Francisco, CA 94131
415-643-4300

What if your defenses fail?
CYBER BREACH
Designing an exercise to map a ready strategy

Copyright © 2016 by **Regina Phelps**

All rights reserved. No part of this book may be reproduced or transmitted in any form or by any means, electronic or mechanical, including but not limited to photocopying, analog or digital recording, or by any use of an information storage and retrieval system without the publisher's written permission, except by a reviewer who may quote brief passages in a review to be printed or published in a magazine, newspaper or on the Internet.

Published by:
  Chandi Media
  260 Whitney Street
  San Francisco, CA 94131
  415-643-4300
  www.ChandiMedia.com
  Info@ChandiMedia.com

Although the author and publisher have made every effort to ensure the accuracy and completeness of information contained in this book, we are not liable, directly or indirectly, for any errors, inaccuracies, omissions or any inconsistency herein, nor are we liable in any manner for consequences of any group's or individual's interpretation or implementation of the materials presented.

ISBN: 978-0-9831143-4-5
LCCN: 2016933689

Contents

	Acknowledgements	vii
	Preface	ix
1	Why conduct cyber exercises?	1
2	Eight things you must have to make this exercise rock!	9
3	Before you start this!	17
4	What type of exercise? It has to be simulated!	23
5	Not one, but two Design Teams	31
6	The starting point: The exercise plan	43
7	What drives the story? The narrative	57
8	Moving the exercise forward — Exercise injects	67
9	Make your exercises "public" for greater impact	83
10	The team makes it happen, the Exercise Team	91
11	Leading up to the Big Day!	103
12	Game Day!	115
13	Writing the after-action report!	131
14	Now what? Exercise follow-up	143
	Glossary	147
	Appendix	157

Acknowledgements and gratitude

"Silent gratitude isn't much use to anyone."
— *G.B. Stern*

I am grateful for my many clients around the world and, in particular, those we have worked with to meet this new cyber challenge. In developing cyber exercises with these organizations, I came to better understand the challenges and issues they might face. And then in the actual exercises, I saw them work through the difficulties to build an effective response where there had been none.

I am grateful to my editor, Meg Keehan, for her efforts in smoothing out the edges of my writing and filling in mysterious gaps. I greatly appreciate my colleague, Kelly Williams, who shared his technology expertise and knowledge to make this a better book.

And lastly, I am very grateful to my husband, Dave Kieffer. I could not ask for a more loving, caring and supportive partner. A former consultant, he helps with research and editing. He also supports me while I am on the road and loves me through it all. I am blessed and deeply thankful.

I hope you find this book helpful and that your exercises help your organization to be better prepared for the significant challenges ahead.

Let me know how you are doing,

Regina Phelps
Regina@ems-solutionsinc.com

Preface

In my professional practice, I have had the privilege of leading over 100 exercises a year for over 30 years. Most of these exercises have been for large multi-national companies. In recent years, I have found conducting cyber exercises to be some of the most sobering experiences for fairly simple reasons:

- ▶ A cyber attack is a threat that all companies and organizations face. Yet, virtually no one is ready for one.
- ▶ While organizations are feverishly working to fend off a cyber attack, very few have a plan for the impact of an actual attack.
- ▶ If an attack happens, it can be devastating.
- ▶ There are very few risks that executives and boards fear more.
- ▶ The chance of it happening to most any organization is very, very high. The only question is how bad it will be?

In my mind, those are pretty compelling reasons to use a cyber scenario for your next company exercise.

An exercise with a cyber scenario has obvious risks. Some may fear people – from investors to hackers – may hear about it. Some will blame IT leaders. Some may lament insufficient budgets. It must not be turned into a blame game. The goal is to get all of the facts, issues and concerns into the open and expose weaknesses and vulnerabilities *now*, so something can be done about them *now*.

What I've learned from doing so many exercises over the years is that — with a bit of careful planning, creativity, and vision — a great exercise can be devised that will really help build a company's plan, program, and team.

And it will certainly foster confidence throughout the organization.

Helping you build *your* plan, program, and team is what this book is all about.

Regina Phelps
San Francisco, California

CHAPTER ONE

Why conduct cyber exercises?

Chapter goals:
1. Learn what an exercise is.
2. Discover eight benefits of conducting a cyber exercise.
3. Know at least eight reasons to do a cyber exercise.
4. Identify the four outcomes of a successful exercise.
5. Understand how often you should do an exercise to have a competent plan and team.

What is an exercise?

An exercise is a *simulation* of the performance of duties, tasks, and operations in a manner that is very similar to the way they would be performed in a real incident. An exercise is an activity designed to promote business and management preparedness. During an exercise, I ask people to imagine that this is a movie, a play, or a book. The exercise creates an experience and then places people into that experience where we can observe how they perform.

Every month we read about the latest, the biggest, or "the most significant cyber breach ever." It has practically become a "breach a day," each one more significant, larger, greater, and more catastrophic than the one before. Companies are jostling to figure out how to manage these challenging cyber security issues, and it's not just IT that's scrambling. Cyber incidents affect every aspect of the business, and cyber security has become one of the most pressing issues in business continuity management today.

Cyber exercise benefits

If you have elected to read this book, I am probably preaching to the choir. However, it is likely you may need to convince your organization's management, your colleagues, or your boss as to why you should conduct a cyber exercise. So what are the benefits of having an exercise with a cyber security scenario? There are eight of them:

- ▶ Define the roles and responsibilities of the team(s) tasked with managing a cyber incident. For example, what do the information security, incident management, and executive teams do in a cyber incident?
- ▶ Evaluate communication between all of the different groups and teams that will suddenly get plunged into a crisis. Many of these links have not been clearly mapped out in the context of a cyber incident.
- ▶ Assess the adequacy of current procedures and policies in the context of a cyber incident. (Spoiler alert: They will likely be woefully inadequate.)
- ▶ Develop an impact plan for a cyber incident. We call this "Plan B." Everyone is putting all of their attention and dollars on prevention, which is good and important; but virtually no one is preparing for the impact after it has happened. You need a Plan B cyber impact plan, and then you need to practice it.
- ▶ Assist in the evaluation of cyber insurance needs. This is a hot new emerging market. What kind of coverage do you have? Does the insurance company have specific requirements of what should or should not be done? Does the incident management team know what these do's and don'ts are so their actions don't nullify the coverage?
- ▶ Map the big decisions. There are a lot of big decisions that need to be made and it is likely that they have not been documented. Who can authorize a disconnect from the Internet? What are the criteria to do so (and have the procedures for doing so been defined)? What about the core network? Those are just some of the big questions that need to be raised and answered.
- ▶ Educate executives about the threat and engage them in their role during a cyber incident.
- ▶ Shine a light on the "cyber Bogeyman[1]" and help you clearly see

---

1   Bogeyman: is a common allusion to a mythical creature in many cultures used by adults or older children to frighten bad children into good behavior. It is simply a non-specific embodiment of terror. Wikipedia: https://en.wikipedia.org/wiki/Bogeyman

what is needed to get ready. At this point, it is not a matter of if your company will be hacked, only a matter of when

Let's look at these eight benefits in a little more depth.

1. Develop the roles and responsibilities during the cyber incident

Who does what during a cyber incident? Who are the "big players" in this situation? There will likely be a lot of assumptions made at this time and that could lead to confusion and chaos when calm and clarity are needed. Likely response teams may include IT Incident Response, Information Security, Corporate Incident Management, Joint Information Center, Business Department Operations Centers (DOCs), and Executives. Who does what and when? An exercise will help you work that out.

2. Evaluate communication among all of the different groups and teams

In the heat of the cyber incident is **NOT** the time to figure out who notifies who and who calls whom. These communications must clearly be defined in advance. Because a cyber incident may involve more players than a 'normal' incident, knowing who the players are and mapping out the communication between and among them are key. Then those communication points need to be exercised.

3. Assess the adequacy of current procedures and policies

It is very likely that your current procedures, processes, and policies will fall quite short. After all, this is a new phenomenon. In all of the cyber exercises EMSS has done, many of which with very large multi-national corporations, we have not yet found one with plans that would suffice in a cyber incident.

4. Develop an impact plan for a cyber incident, a "Plan B"

Spoiler alert: It's unlikely that you have an impact plan for a cyber incident. Go ahead, pull out the business continuity plans. How long can the company be without its systems? A few hours? A few days? What if it were down for a week? What about two weeks - or more - before your systems were back up and running? And what if the recovery point objective [2] is 24 hours, but the system restore process has to go back weeks or months?

Once you develop Plan B, it needs to be practiced, exercised. "Muscle memory" needs to be developed. Human nature tells us that people don't pull out plans when the crisis hits, they go on instinct. Yes, they will *eventually* pull out the plans, but their gut reactions will kick in first. Plans are important for the preparation that goes into them, but exercises build effective responses. That is what a team needs and wants when crisis strikes, and exercises will help them develop that muscle memory with practice, practice, practice.

5. *Assist you to evaluate cyber insurance needs*

Cyber insurance is the new big hot thing. But what kind of coverage do you need and what does the insurance company expect of you during a cyber incident? A recent Wells Fargo survey[3] of 100 U.S. middle-market and large companies found that 85% say they have purchased cyber and data privacy insurance, while 44% have already filed a claim as a result of a breach.

An exercise can help you evaluate your cyber insurance needs. Most states now require companies to notify customers if there is a data breach. Does yours? Within what parameters? Cybercrime is also a growing concern in the boardrooms of publicly-traded companies, where the questions often asked include, "Do we have enough coverage? Do we have the right coverage?"

6. *Map the big decisions*

There many big decisions that need to be made and frankly, a lot of them have never really been thought about, let alone documented. When a breach first occurs, executives may think that the safest thing is to disconnect from the Internet. The rationale of doing this is to "stop the bleeding." But who has the authority to disconnect the company from the Internet? What are the implications of doing that? What happens when the company has no web-

---

2   Recovery Point Objective: Defines the maximum tolerable data loss that is acceptable in a disaster situation. https://www.symantec.com/security_response/glossary/define.jsp%3Fletter%3Dr%26word%3Drecovery-point-objective-rpo

3   "Wells Fargo 2015 Cyber Security and Data Privacy Survey: How prepared are you?" https://wfis.wellsfargo.com/insights/research/2015-Cyber-Security-and-Data-Privacy-Survey/Documents/Cyber_data_privacy_survey_white_paper_FNL.pdf

site or on-line sales capability? No email? Maybe even no phones?

Similarly, what if someone wants to cut the internal core network to stop these infections from spreading around the company systems? How would this impact the business units and their ability to work? Would the organization still be able to function?

It is important to use an exercise to begin deep discussions on some of these big issues. A cyber exercise will fully engage everyone in working out the best responses to these critical questions and decisions.

7. Educate executives about the threat and engage them in their role during a cyber incident

Many executives will simply point to the Information Security folks and say, "Don't let this happen!" but they don't really understand what "it" is. An exercise clearly demonstrates what "it" is and how bad "it" could get. EMSS has seen many instances where, following an exercise, the internal IT exercise Design Team met with the executives and deeply explained how the scenario could or would have happened. This is incredibly powerful after the executives have gone through the exercise and experienced the (virtual) pain of how the situation ended up. It gives them a clearer understanding of how it could happen. This may even create for you, one or more champions for life.

8. Shine a light on the "cyber Bogeyman"

I am a huge fan of bringing the scary thing into the light. We all hear about cyber attacks and breaches, and our imaginations can run wild with how bad they can be. But once you have gone through the situation virtually during an exercise, it seems more manageable. All of that is good for planing, team development, and confidence.

A pessimist sees the difficulty in every opportunity.
An optimist sees the opportunity in every difficulty.
— ***Winston Churchill***

Exercise outcomes

What can you tell your management team when they ask you, "So, what are we going to get out of doing a cyber exercise?" There are at least four powerful answers:
1. Advance overall company readiness.
2. Improve the business continuity management system within the company.
3. Provide individual training.
4. Facilitate plan updates.

Advance overall company readiness

There are only two ways to know if your plans are going to work. One way is to experience a cyber incident and just see how it goes. The second is to conduct an exercise with a cyber scenario in advance. In virtually all organizations the preferred method would be the latter. It is a lot more effective to have an exercise to determine how your plans will work, and it's infinately less stressful! An exercise also gives you the chance to go back and change the plans as needed without the pain of going through a real cyber attack.

Improve the incident management and continuity program within the company

Every exercise improves your Incident Management Team and Business Continuity plans and teams. Plans are written in a vacuum. It is only when you practice them that they come to life and you can clearly see what works and what needs improvement.

Provide individual training

As we all know, adults learn best by doing, not by reading a book or reviewing a plan. If you want your incident team to know what to do when a cyber incident happens, you need to practice it in advance and actually *"live"* the experience.

Facilitate plan updates

The overall goal of an exercise is to wind up with an up-to-date plan. Once an exercise has concluded, you will know the areas of the plan that need to be modified and improved. The revisions that occur after every exercise continue to refine the plan and keep it "battle ready."

> *If we all did the things we are capable of doing, we would literally astound ourselves."*
> — *Thomas Edison*

How often do you need to conduct an exercise?

EMSS recommends doing a cyber exercise at least once a year; more often if your company's cyber-response capabilities are new or are known to be inadequate. The threat landscape is changing daily and your team needs to keep up. To build a solid team, twice a year is recommended. One exercise can be a more challenging exercise (Advanced Tabletop, Functional or Full-scale exercise) and the other can be more of a conversation (Basic Tabletop).

In the private-sector, most companies, thankfully, have relatively few plan activations. That is, of course, good, but it also means that the teams aren't very well practiced. This also means that a good exercise program may provide the team with the only chance they have to practice their plan and procedures.

My experience is that teams are pretty green for their first few cyber exercises. But around exercise number three – providing the team remains relatively stable from exercise to exercise – they really begin to gel as a team and the plan has been shaken out fairly well. As the old maxim goes, "Practice makes perfect."

The exercise glossary

Throughout the book, I use terms that you may not be familiar with, such as "exercise players" or "exercise injects." This might be a good time to check out and familiarize yourself with the terms and definitions in the glossary. It might make your reading the rest of the book a tad easier and less confusing

Summary

A cyber incident is very likely in your future. It is complicated and has many twists and turns. To get ready, you must exercise your teams. This book will tell you who *needs to participate*, what *types of issues* you will face, what kinds of *plans you will need*, and what *types of decisions* will need to be made.

CHAPTER TWO

Eight things you must have to make this exercise rock!

Chapter goals
1. Learn what makes a cyber exercise different and so impactful.
2. See the difference between a routine emergency and a crisis emergency.
3. Identify the eight things you need to have in place to make this exercise a success.

Nowadays, a cyber incident seems to be every company's greatest fear. Not only is there confidential company or customer information that could be exposed, these events are stunningly expensive on many levels: The costs to:
- ▶ Detect the problem in the first place.
- ▶ Determine what data was compromised (or lost).
- ▶ Recover the data if necessary, compensate customers for actual or potential damages.
- ▶ General cost of disruption to the business.
- ▶ And, of course, this does not take into account the damage to a company's reputation and loss of current and future business.

In 2014, the Ponemon Institute found the average annual cost of responding to cyber attacks was $12.7 million, up 96 percent over the previous five years.[4] There are also the high profile and expensive losses such as Target $148 million or Home Depot $62 million.

Companies are spending millions of dollars to prevent these attacks from occurring, which is a wise and prudent investment. No one, however, seems to be talking about how to deal with the impact of such a breach once

---

4 "Cost of Cyber Attacks Jumps for US Firms: Study", Security Week, October 2014 http://www.securityweek.com/cost-cyber-attacks-jumps-us-firms-study

it has occurred. We have surveyed our clients, professional colleagues, and other firms, and in our small sample size, we found that no one is planning for the *impact* of a cyber attack.

In the past couple of years, we have done numerous exercises on the impact of a cyber breach, and have found them to be effective, thought-provoking exercises. Do you want to get your executives and incident management team ready for such a cyber attack? Then put these issues and considerations out on the table. It is no longer an abstraction or theoretical. It is real. An exercise will set the state for needed strategic and tactical discussions and changes.

This chapter is a quick overview of what we think you need to have in place to make this exercise a success. Subsequent chapters will peel this overview back in more detail.

What makes a cyber scenario so different?

One of the things I often hear continuity professionals say is that they "plan for the worse-case scenario." Whenever I hear that, I immediately stop them. This is simply not true. You don't plan for the worse-case scenario; you plan for what may be bad but is still a "routine" emergency. There is not enough time, money, or risk tolerance to plan for worse-case scenarios.

"Routine" emergency

To be clear, routine emergency[5] does not mean "easy." A routine emergency can still be difficult and challenging. In this context, "routine" refers to the relative predictability of the situation that permits advanced preparation. This risk is in the company's risk profile and the company has likely been able to take advantage of lessons learned from prior experiences. It is more likely that these situations have been thought about and planned for. The requirements are known and training and exercises have probably been done. Most incident management, crisis communications, business continuity, and disaster recovery plans are filled with strategies to manage routine emergencies.

---

5   *Managing Crisis: Responses to Large-Scale Emergencies*, Arnold Howitt and Herman Leonard, CQ Press, page 5

"Crisis" emergency

A crisis emergency[6] is a much different animal. These types of events are distinguished by significant elements of novelty. This novelty makes the problem much more difficult to predict, diagnosis and then deal with. This type of emergency can have the following characteristics:

- ▶ The threats have never been encountered before, therefore there are no plans to manage it.
- ▶ It may be a familiar event, however, it is occurring at unprecedented speed, therefore developing an appropriate response is severely challenging.
- ▶ There may be a confluence of forces, which, while not new individually, in combination, pose unique challenges to the response.

The novel nature of a crisis emergency becomes a game-changer. Plans, processes and procedures, training, and exercises that may work well in routine emergency situations are frequently grossly inadequate in a crisis emergency, and may even be counterproductive. Very often, you have to start from scratch.

The crisis emergency requires different capabilities. In other words, the plans and behaviors used for routine emergencies will not work. The first thing to do is to identify the elements of the novelty and determine what makes this situation so different from others. In a cyber attack or breach, this novelty is often surprising. The process may begin with thinking the situation is one thing — perhaps almost routine — and then over time, realize it is something quite different. For example, a situation may seem like it's a routine technology problem or outage, and then over time, it is revealed to be something more significant and sinister.

Once the real problem has been identified and reality sets in that those plans won't work, improvised response measures that will be suitable to cope with the unanticipated aspects of the incident need to be developed. In other words, this is new territory; this hasn't been covered before. Created out of necessity, these responses may be actions quite different from those ever done before. Handling a crisis emergency may feel like building an airplane while flying it at the same time. It's not pretty, but it may be necessary.

---

6   Ibid, page 6.

Lastly, in a crisis emergency, the response must be creative, and, *at the same time*, be extremely adaptable when it is being executed. Companies must be on "full alert" at all times, as the situation can change on a moment's notice, and the response team must be prepared to shift very quickly. All of this makes people quite anxious, and during an exercise, this anxiety often manifests itself in varying degrees of excessively loud voices or hushed voices, frantic activities, and nervous laughter.

> *Before anything else, preparation is the key to success.*
> — *Alexander Graham Bell*

Eight design aspects you must consider in this exercise

To manage this very different type of exercise, you need to have eight things in place to make it work:

1. **Senior management support** *(see Chapter 3)*
   Right off the bat, senior management needs to understand that this exercise is likely to produce many learnings and issues that will need to be resolved after the exercise is over. It will also present topics that they probably have never thought about or deeply understood. This could easily make people feel uncomfortable with quite a few unanswered questions at the end of the experience. As you explore the topic, you will likely also need to provide some cover for the Technology and Information Security departments so the exercise doesn't turn into a blame game or a witch hunt.

2. **A willing technology and information security department** *(see Chapter 3)*
   The Technology and Information Security Departments need to be an active planner in the exercise. You'll need several excellent staff members from those departments to be a key part of the design process. They cannot be players on the response team who are being exercised. You need them to help determine what the cause of the scenario breach will be. When you first begin, this will undoubtedly make them uncomfortable,

because in the back of their mind, they are afraid they will be blamed in some way. You'll need to reassure them that that's not the goal of the exercise.

Once you've identified your key design team participants, the first question you will need to ask them is, "Could we be hacked?" The answer will inevitably be "yes." The next question is, "How could that happen?" The list is long but could include things such as phishing, watering holes, or infected flash drives. You just need to find a likely means; you don't need a deep exploration of the intrusion. Be aware that you may need to provide them some cover too!

3. **The right exercise type** *(See Chapter 4)*
There are three types of exercises that can be used with a cyber narrative: Advanced Tabletop, Functional, or Full Scale[7]. What these styles have in common is a Simulation Team. This type of exercise requires a Simulation Team to make it work. Why? The teams going through the experience need to have someone to interact with to solve the problems. How does it work? An exercise player receives new information (an "exercise inject") and to solve the problem, he needs to speak to a simulator. The simulator may not agree with the answer. S/he may think it doesn't solve the problem or s/he could have many other responses. In other words, the Simulation Team member causes our exercise player to think more deeply about a response and will therefore will have to rethink their plan and response. Because of that the exercise player will have a deeper and more valuable experience.

4. **Two design teams** *(see Chapter 5)*
You will need two Design Teams: An IT/Information Security Design Team and a "standard" exercise Design Team. The IT/Info Sec team needs to do a deep dive on the narrative and develop the timeline of issues that happened before the exercise's scenario date. They will also need to provide a very detailed timeline of what will be happening during the exercise. Once they have developed the breach timeline, the

---

[7] *Emergency Management Exercises*, Regina Phelps, Chandi Media, http://tinyurl.com/pyt9p8x and see this books glossary.

other Design Team can begin to develop their injects.

The standard Design Team should include participants from key lines of business, human resources, communications, facilities, security, and any other in-scope lines of business and departments. Those team members should take the cyber narrative and timeline, and develop their injects, which will tell the story of the IT problems from their perspective. Remember, in an exercise, if you don't tell the players what's happening, they don't know what's going on and will invent things. The injects are the way you tell them the story.

5. **Interwoven narrative and injects** (see Chapters 7 and 8)
The narrative for this exercise will have lots of sometimes arcane facts and circumstances. It has a certainly complexity that can't be avoided. The story progresses through the injects, and the injects must "dance" with the cyber narrative. The exercise players have to tease the information apart, work with the Simulators to figure out what's going on, and then improvise a plan. When they develop that plan, then the Simulators have to adapt to the new plan and, in some cases, create new injects "on the fly" to make it all work. The narrative and the injects are constantly ebbing and flowing together to tell the entire story.

6. **Make it public – "out" the company** (see Chapter 9)
One of the key aspects of this narrative is the potential damage to the reputation of the company. To damage that reputation, you have to "out" the company in the exercise narrative. We recommend doing this early in the exercise by having the "perpetrator" post the story on a social media platform such as Twitter. (NOTE: Of course, this is not a real Tweet. This is all done via "exercise magic.") To add a sense of reality, EMSS will often have our Media team produce videos in a similar style as a hacker video, such as those done by Anonymous[8]. These kinds of videos make the experience for the players far more realistic.

To make it even more interesting, we then create a second video from one of the local news stations, with the report announcing the station is

---

8   *Anonymous* YouTube channel https://www.youtube.com/user/AnonymousWorldvoce

on its way to the company under siege seeking official comments and interviews with executives. Mission accomplished – company outed! The players then have to deal with the fallout There is no brushing the event under the rug.

7. *A well-honed after-action report* *(see Chapter 13)*
Due to the political issues with this exercise, the After-action Report (AAR) needs to be written carefully. It needs to present what was discovered in a very positive light. After all, now that you know what doesn't work or what you don't have, you can fix it. The AAR will likely be viewed by executives, boards, auditors, and others. There may be several versions of this report that you might prepare:
- ▶ Executive Summary for executives: a short summary of the findings and observations[9].
- ▶ Detailed AAR for the teams that need to resolve the issues.
- ▶ Special section reports (for particular departments) to highlight findings and what they need to do to correct them.
- ▶ Regulatory/audit version: This version maybe something in-between a short Executive Summary and a detailed AAR.

8. *Careful exercise follow-up* *(see Chapter 14)*
This exercise will likely reveal many, many issues, and, no doubt, many of them will be identified as "Urgent!" You know you can't fix everything at once. You need a careful plan of attack to get through all of the likely action items. Here are a few things to think about:
- ▶ Get the report in front of the right people for acknowledgement and support.
- ▶ Develop a detailed punch list and prioritize. Get the right people to agree on the priorities.
- ▶ Strike while the iron is hot. Executives and business leaders want to resolve these issues and funding may become more available for this than anything else

---

9   When writing AARs we never use the word 'recommendations,' but rather use 'observations.' Many of our clients are in regulated industries and the word "recommendation" implies that they *must* do what we are saying, which gives them no opportunity to modify the observation for their particular situation.

> *However beautiful the strategy,*
> *you should occasionally look at the results.*
> — *Winston Churchill*

Summary

For businesses, the risk of experiencing a data breach is higher than ever with almost half of organizations suffering at least one security incident in the last 12 months.[10] The C-suite and Board members are very aware of the effect that a data breach can have on company's reputation. In addition, consumers are demanding more communication and remedies from businesses after a data breach occurs.

If the future is anything like the past, cyber incidents are not going away anytime soon. Life will continue to be even more complicated. Plan your next exercise to be a cyber exercise. Focus it on the impact of a breach and *how your organization will deal with it*. Based on the probability of a cyber event, you had better get going!

---

10 "Data Breach and Industry Forecast 2015", Experian http://www.experian.com/assets/data-breach/white-papers/2015-industry-forecast-experian.pdf

CHAPTER THREE

Before starting, you need this!

Chapter goals:
1. Understand the importance of senior management support.
2. Identify ways to avoid the "blame game."
3. Learn the importance of having willing Technology and Information Security departments.
4. Get the Technology department to be a committed partner in the exercise design.

The role of senior management support and a willing Technology and Information Security Department

There are two things that you must have in place before you begin to make this planning process and exercise go smoothly. Both are critically important. You need senior management commitment and you need a willing Technology and Information Security department.

"Cyber threats are an urgent and growing danger."
— ***President Barack Obama,*** *January 2015*

Senior Management and cyber risk

A wide-range of cyber risks have emerged in recent years and clearly no company or organization is immune. And just when you think you understand them, the threats morph, evolve, and change. High-profile losses of data stored on portable devices are growing. The Internet is producing new schemes that we could hardly imagine just a few years ago. What's next? Governments are stepping up their involvement to implement laws which will hold the controllers and "holders" of data to higher standards in terms of cyber risk.

These issues can have serious consequences from a legal, regulatory, and financial perspective. Cyber risk has, therefore, rapidly evolved from being a peripheral area of concern into a critical core business issue, which should deeply involve senior management and those at the Board level.

> *"Houston, we've had a problem here."*
> — ***The crew of the Apollo 13***[11]

Senior Management responsibilities

Senior management is subject to a number of obligations and duties, whether by specific regulations or legal statutes. These individuals have a duty to act in the best interests of the company and must ensure that the company has proper policies and procedures in place, as well as adequate systems and controls.

When a cyber incident occurs, the spotlight can quickly turn to senior managers and the role they play in securing the company's valuable information. The brand and reputation of the company is at stake, and it will be tried in the court of public opinion. Affected third parties that suffer a loss may look to the company to recover their losses. These claims may allege senior management's breach-of-duty of care or breach of confidence arising out of a loss of data. Board members can also be exposed to shareholder actions for breach-of-duty if a cyber risk is not mitigated and a cyber incident causes a drop in the share price.

Senior managers need to understand the risks and the potential liabilities they face as a result of cyber risk and get engaged not only in prevention but also in the crisis management role once an incident has occurred. Senior management must understand:
- ▶ Their role during a cyber security incident.
- ▶ The cyber risk that the company is facing.
- ▶ If the appropriate cyber security and risk mitigation measures have been put in place to deal with the cyber risk that has been identified.

---

11 The origin can be traced to the phrase in past tense ("Houston, we've had a problem here") that was used by the crew of the Apollo 13 moon flight, to report a major technical problem back to Houston. The phrase is normally misquoted as "Houston, we have a problem". Wiktionary: https://en.wiktionary.org/wiki/Houston,_we_have_a_problem

Cybersecurity is a CEO-level issue

A recent whitepaper by Tucker Bailey, James Kaplan, and Chris Rezek entitled, "Why senior leaders are the front line against cyberattacks" hit the nail right on the head: "Cybersecurity is a CEO-level issue. The risks of cyberattacks span functions and business units, companies and customers. And given the stakes and the challenging decisions posed by becoming cyberresilient, making the decisions necessary can only be achieved with active engagement from the CEO and other members of the senior-management team."[12]

A well-designed cyber exercise will help to educate senior management and engage them further in the issues of both prevention and response.

A good leader takes a little more than his share of the blame, a little less than his share of the credit.
— *Arnold H. Glasgow*

The "no blame game" rule

One of the most important actions you need to take before you get too involved in exercise design and planning is to get senior management buy in. What this really means is that you want to make *sure* that they understand what is likely to happen during the exercise. This is key because when things get really messy, and there doesn't seem to be a solution in sight (as will happen during a cyber scenario exercise), there should be no blame assigned to *anyone*.

The only way this exercise works is by everyone understanding that (a) there is a lot to learn in the exercise, (b) the exercise will be messy, and (c) everyone is working hard to prevent and respond to such an incident. There are likely many initiatives and lots of dollars being spent on cyber issues, and some executives might have a tendency to say something like, "How could this happen?" or "We've spent so much money and we still aren't safe?" or "How could (fill in the name) let this happen?"

You can't have that. You have to go "all in" and be ready to learn and

---
[12] *Why senior leaders are the front line against cyberattacks*, by Tucker Bailey, James Kaplan, and Chris Rezek, McKinsey & Company, June 2014.

suffer and grow together. The only way that works is if there is no blame.

> *When you blame others, you give up your power to change.*
> —*Robert Anthony*

A willing Technology and Information Security Department

Having willing Technology and Information Security departments participating in a cyber exercise cannot be understated. If you're not careful, this exercise can turn into a high-stakes game for the Technology and Information Security departments and, in particular, Technology management. After all, "the problem" is happening in their shop. And some people might look at them with a "Why did you let this happen?" look. Therefore, they have to be willing to go along with the scenario, *and* you might have to provide them cover.

The Technology and Information Security Departments need to provide you with people who can design the "air-tight" storyline. This Technology Exercise Design Team will be essential in spelling out how the supposed breach occurred. They are being asked to expose the company's soft underbelly, disclose possible weaknesses, and then help drive the spear into them. This may make them nervous.

I personally think about this as a fabulous opportunity for everyone in the company to learn and appreciate the ever-growing complexities that the IT team faces. Only when all of the issues are out in the open, solutions can be found. If fixes aren't possible, then discovering workarounds and ways to tighten response and impact plans are good to know.

I encourage you to meet with Technology management to describe the exercise design process, emphasize the critical importance of their participation and having the right people on the Technology Exercise Design Team. You likely will need people who know "everything" about the technology systems: infrastructure, networks, applications, databases, and storage. This may be one person or it may be five. In any case, they will be your key designers. It is also important that these individuals not be participating as an exercise player. More about this in the Chapter Five.

*Willingness to change is a strength,
even if it means plunging part of the company
into total confusion for a while.*
— *Jack Welch*

Summary

Building senior and technology management engagement is critical in an exercise with this scenario. Begin at the top first, build commitment and buy-in, and you will be off to a great exercise design start.

CHAPTER FOUR

What type of exercise? It has to be simulated!

> *Chapter goals:*
> 1. Identify the five different types of exercises.
> 2. Know which three of those five types will yield the best result for a cyber scenario.
> 3. Understand the importance of a Simulation Team in a cyber exercise.
> 4. Learn what is involved with an Advanced Tabletop, Functional, and Full-scale exercise.
> 5. Present "typical" agendas for an Advanced Tabletop, Functional, and Full-scale exercise

Types of exercises[13]

There are five basic exercise types:
1. Orientation (including workshops and training)
2. Drill.
3. Tabletop (including Basic and Advanced)
4. Functional
5. Full-scale

A cyber exercise can be any one of these three:
1. Tabletop (Advanced)
2. Functional
3. Full-scale

Any one of these three will work well because they all involve the use of a Simulation Team. Simulation Teams are an integral part of the exercise:

---
13 All of these exercise types are discussed at length in our book *Emergency Management Exercises: From Response to Recovery,* Dec 2010, available on Amazon.

Simulation Team members deliver the injects, they interact with the exercise players, and they can also act as the "outside world" - all critical activities to make this exercise seem real and work.

Why is the Simulation Team element so important?

All exercises are, of course, a world of "make believe," a simulation. You create this hypothetical environment and then drop the players into it. Then they have to figure out what is going on (gain situational awareness) and plot a course of action. A cyber exercise is even more challenging because the players can't go to a computer or device to see what is going on. If the scenario has caused the company website to be vandalized, have files disappear, corrupt backups, or caused the network to run painfully slow, the only way they know that it's happened is by someone telling them. While it's true that that's what an exercise inject does, to really play out the story, you need someone the players can talk to so they better understand more of the problem and can engage in a back-and-forth dialogue.

When conducting technology-based exercises, we've had a player announce more than once, "We fixed it!" when an inject tells them, for example, that a server has died. On the design side of the narrative, we knew a fix wasn't possible, so there needs to be someone to say right back them, "No, you haven't!" That is what a simulation team does!

In summary, a Simulation Team:
- ▶ Tells the story via injects.
- ▶ Gives the players someone to talk with and solve a problem.
- ▶ Pushes back when the players have a solution that won't work for the scenario. ("That server will not come back up, regardless of what we do!")
- ▶ Causes the players to think more deeply about the solution/answer and the problem.

Without a Simulation Team, it is very difficult to get the players to think more deeply about the problem. In an Orientation or Basic Tabletop exercise, the players simply state what they would do to fix the problem, and that's pretty much it. There is no one to push back. No one to say "it didn't work." And no one to challenge an answer.

A Simulation Team makes the exercise players think, and will make your team and its plans better and stronger.

> *Acting is like a Halloween mask that you put on.*
> — **River Phoenix**

Which exercise type should you start with?

Keep in mind that team or plan development is an evolutionary activity. All of the learning and planning is truly incremental. The normal progression is to start the team's development with an Orientation exercise, then progress to a Tabletop, then onto a Functional exercise, and then, perhaps, a Full-scale exercise. This progression is an opportunity to watch your team mature, with each step along the way designed to build their skills and confidence.

If your team is brand new and has never done an exercise, start with an orientation exercise using a simple narrative like a fire or power outage. This allows them to work out the issues of what their role is, how they work together and other critical activities. Then progress to a basic tabletop with another narrative.[14] Then your team would be ready for a cyber incident.

TYPES OF EXERCISES USING SIMULATION TEAM		
ADVANCED TABLETOP	**FUNCTIONAL**	**FULL-SCALE**
More realistic than orientation or "basic" tabletops	Very realistic, injects are delivered by phone or other media and feels very real	Very realistic, injects are delivered by phone or other media AND includes a field response (such as going to an alternate work site, recovery area or back data center)
Changes the narrative with injects	Includes more complex and sophisticated injects and requires exercise players to perform certain activities (without actually deploying them)	Involves more complex detail, often hundreds of injects and the expectation that they will be deployment if necessary to solve the inject

---

14 Ibid

TYPES OF EXERCISES USING SIMULATION TEAM		
ADVANCED TABLETOP	**FUNCTIONAL**	**FULL-SCALE**
Uses a simulation team to interact with the players	Larger exercise team in general: designers, simulators, and observers	Larger exercise team in general: designers, simulators, observers and exercise assistants
Takes about two months to plan	Takes at last three months to plan	Takes six or more months to plan
Requires at least three hours of time	Requires at least four hours	Requires at least six to eight hours
Least costly option	Increased cost due to size, media and equipment required	The most expensive exercise

Advanced tabletop exercise

Tabletop exercises are by far the most common and frequently performed exercise. Most continuity professionals, however, do a Basic Tabletop.

▶ Basic Tabletop: Seeks to solve problems in a group setting via discussion and brainstorming. There may be some injects, but they are all dealt with in a simple discussion format.

▶ Advanced Tabletop: Includes the introduction of injects and an exercise Simulation Team acting as proxies for the outside world.

EMSS came up with the idea of an Advanced Tabletop in the mid-1990s[15]. I noticed how teams would solve problems during exercises. Team members would be presented with a narrative and a series of assumptions and artificialities, and they were asked to come up with a solution. In most cases, the teams would snap their fingers and – amazingly! – they always got what they wanted. They were not really dealing with issues and complicated factors that were facing them, such as not having enough equipment, running out of diesel fuel or water, or having insufficient staff. I felt that the teams would not be able to build a solid plan or have a great team if they were never challenged, so I introduced the concept of a Simulation Team into the experience.

In an Advanced Tabletop exercise, a small Simulation Team (the number of team members will vary based on the size of the exercise) portrays various members of the outside world, such as "Emergency Responders," "Media,"

---

15 We started doing these in the mid-90s. I don't know if we invented them but I don't know anyone else that does them!

"Contractors/Vendors," or my favorite, "Genius-of-all-Trades" (Sim Team members who can play anybody).[16]

> *"All the world's a stage."*
> — **William Shakespeare** *(As You Like It)*

ADVANCED TABLETOP EXERCISE SAMPLE AGENDA		
ACTIVITY	**TIME**	**DISCUSSION LEADER**
Welcome and Introductions	9:00 AM – 9:10 AM	Senior executive
Tabletop exercise	9:10 AM – 12:00 PM	Exercise facilitator
Short break - grab lunch	12:00 PM – 12:10 PM	
Debrief over lunch	12:10 PM - 12:45 PM	Exercise facilitator
Next steps	12:50 PM – 1:00 PM	Senior executive

Functional Exercise

Functional exercises are fully simulated and feel very realistic. This means that participants perform all activities (within the confines of the exercise environment, no field deployment), all exercise injects are delivered via telephone by a Simulator and there are audio and/or video broadcasts. During a Functional exercise, you could walk into the exercise environment and within a few moments you would swear that this event was really happening.

In this type of exercise, there are a significant number of injects delivered by the Simulation Team to provide that realistic give-and-take that makes the event seem real. This exercise also has a larger cast of characters on the day of the event (more Simulators and Observers), and needs a bigger Design Team for planning the exercise. This exercise also requires more equipment, with all injects being delivered by phone, emails, mock news reports or other means.

---

16 I used to call this role "Jack-" or "Jill-of-all-Trades." However, as a Mac user since 1984, in recent years, I changed it to "Genius-of-all-Trades," in deference to Apple and their "Geniuses," who can answer tech problems.

Functional Exercise

FUNCTIONAL EXERCISE AGENDA/ SAMPLE ONE		
ACTIVITY	TIME	LEADER
Emergency notification system alert to Initial Assessment Team	7:45 AM	
Initial Assessment Team convene	8:00 AM	
Exercise One	8:30 AM – 11:30 AM	
Lunch break (maybe give them an assignment depending on what is going on)	111:30 AM– 12:15 PM	
Exercise Two	12:15 PM – 2:45 PM	
Break	2:45 PM - 3:00 PM	
Debrief (all participants)	3:00 PM - 3:45 PM	
Next steps	3:45 PM - 4:00 PM	

FUNCTIONAL EXERCISE AGENDA/ SAMPLE TWO		
ACTIVITY	TIME	LEADER
Emergency notification system alert to Initial Assessment Team	8:00 AM	
Initial Assessment Team convene	8:30 AM	
Exercise One. Team "A" and Team "B" attend briefing. Team "B" leaves after briefing	9:00 AM – 11:30 AM	
Break for lunch. Both Team "A" and Team "B" attend. During lunch, Team "A" will brief Team "B"	11:30 AM– 12:15 PM	
Exercise Two	12:15 PM – 2:45 PM	
Team "A" returns; Team "B" briefs Team "A"	2:45 PM - 3:00 PM	
Debrief (all participants)	3:00 PM - 3:45 PM	
Next steps	3:45 PM - 4:00 PM	

The Sample One agenda is for a basic exercise with one set of people. The Sample Two agenda demonstrates an exercise with a shift change of personnel. This is often done when the clients' teams are well practiced, and the client is attempting to "right-size" the teams. Since exercises are only done a few times a year, most clients want everyone (primaries and alternates) to participate. That means, of course, that more people would be present in an exercise than would normally be present during a real event. Doing a "shift change" in the exercise allows for "right sizing" the teams to see how they do.

Full-scale Exercise

A Full-scale exercise has all of the complexity of the Functional exercise but with the added layer of an actual field response. In a Full-scale exercise, the exercise players physically go to an alternate site, and/or they may be required to order a resource and actually deploy it.

Note: the type of Full-scale exercise that we facilitate is not to be confused with an annual disaster recovery exercise restoring systems or a business continuity work area recovery exercise that some companies do. Those are less exercise and more "shaking out the bugs," as the leadership simply asks people to do their work or to restore systems at another site. This doesn't really require a narrative, does it?

FULL-SCALE EXERCISE SAMPLE AGENDA		
ACTIVITY	TIME	LEADER
Emergency notification system alert to Initial Assessment Team	7:45 AM	
Initial Assessment Team convene	8:00 AM	

Exercise One. Team "A" and Team "B" attend briefing. Team "B" leaves after briefing
  Executive briefing
  Press conference
	8:30 AM – 11:30 AM
	
	11:00 AM – 11:15 AM
	11:15 AM – 11:30 AM	

Break for lunch. Both Team "A" and Team "B" attend. During lunch, Team "A" will brief Team "B"	11:30 AM– 12:15 PM	
Exercise Two Executive briefing Press conference	12:15 PM – 2:45 PM 2:15 PM – 2:30 PM 2:30 PM – 2:45 PM	
Team "A" returns; Team "B" briefs Team "A"	2:45 PM - 3:00 PM	
Debrief (all participants)	3:00 PM - 3:45 PM	
Next steps	3:45 PM - 4:00 PM	

Summary

Cyber exercises are an evolutionary process. If your team is new, begin by doing an orientation or basic tabletop exercise using a simple narrative such as a fire or power outage. Move on to a cyber narrative using the Advanced Tabletop then grow to a Functional exercise. Some organizations may eventually choose to progress to a Full-scale exercise. It is important to select the appropriate exercise for the maturity level of the team and the plan being exercised.

> *"I always tell the truth. Even when I lie."*
> *— Al Pacino*

CHAPTER FIVE

Not one, but *two* Design Teams

> *Chapter goals:*
> 1. Understand why you need to have two Design Teams.
> 2. Discover the benefits of using Design Teams to create an effective exercise.
> 3. Learn about the types of skills and abilities that you need for each team.
> 4. Identify the likely Design Team players for your exercise.

Design Team basics

EMSS is a strong believer in using exercise Design Teams and a structured Design Team process. You are, indeed, smart, highly capable, and likely know a lot about your company, but you don't know *everything.* And in a cyber scenario exercise, "knowing everything" is even more critical than in a 'normal' exercise. What makes this exercise "spot on" is a highly-tailored narrative and highly-specific injects built around a set of predefined technology and information security incidents. You can't do that alone; you need help. And you don't need just any help, you need the right help. (More about that later.)

There are also notable side benefits to having Design Teams:
- ▶ It is a great way to get more people engaged and excited about the program, the plans, and the processes and procedures. Design Team members become believers, and they share their belief with others.
- ▶ The Design Teams learn so much when they are actively engaged in designing the exercise. They learn about the strengths and weaknesses of the processes and the plans and procedures which then allows them to help make improvements.
- ▶ The insights that the Design Teams gain by being part of the exercise design process can help build awareness about the importance

of business continuity planning. They will also be in a positions to engage and motivate others to make the plans and the program better.

These are all great benefits!

> *If everyone is moving forward together, then success takes care of itself."*
> — **Henry Ford**

What makes a good Exercise Design Team member?

As you are reading this section, you are probably already getting an idea of who would make a good Design Team member. I often find that some people really enjoy being on the design team and will often sign up repeatedly and help design many exercises. When picking Design Team members, look for the following skills and traits:

- ▶ Creative.
- ▶ Detail-oriented.
- ▶ Can think on their own.
- ▶ Can keep a secret.
- ▶ Meets or exceeds deadlines.

Creative

Creative people are open to new and different ideas and can really contribute to and play off the ideas of others. These are folks who can see all colors of the rainbow versus those who can only see black and white. When an idea gets launched in a team meeting, even if it's a bit different or "hasn't happened before," these are the folks who take the idea and run with it -- often coming up with a new twist or angle to a problem.

Meets or exceeds deadlines

Design Team members need to meet or exceed their research or homework targets. One person who lags behind can drag down the whole group and slow your design process to a crawl. Your Design Team members need to work well under pressure and keep on track and on schedule. Don't select someone if they have non-deferrable projects/tasks and/or won't be able to commit to the design schedule.

Detail-oriented

The design process involves coordinating a lot of information, often down to a detailed level ("Which server has that data on it?"). Your team needs to uncover what those details are and research the ramifications within the framework of the exercise. Often, these details hold the keys to the success of your exercise.

Can think on their own

You want people on your team who will question the direction the exercise is going and push back if it doesn't seem to work. (No "'yes' people," please!) Do you remember the concept of "groupthink"? "Groupthink" is a term coined by social psychologist Irving Janis in 1972 after studying historical events, including Pearl Harbor and the Bay of Pigs. The "groupthink" phenomenon occurs when a group makes faulty decisions due to group pressures. These pressures lead to a deterioration of "mental efficiency, reality testing, and moral judgment."[17] Members essentially try to minimize conflict and reach consensus without critically testing, analyzing, and evaluating each others' ideas. Although it isn't always easy to hear, some of my best Design Team members are the ones who will say to me "that's a really silly idea," or "this won't work, and here's why." Those people are invaluable to your design effort.

Can keep a secret

For most exercises, the exercise narrative is should not be divulged in advance; therefore, secrecy is a critical element of in the design process. The reason the narrative is not shared with exercise players is that we want them to come at the problems with fresh eyes and using the plans and procedures that they already have in place. Remember – your Design Team knows all; therefore, they need to be good at keeping exercise specifics to themselves. Team members need to be discreet when conducting their research. Every-

---

17   Janis, Irving L. (1972). *Victims of Groupthink*. New York: Houghton Mifflin.

one knows people who can't keep their mouths shut – those aren't the Design Team members you want!

Are not an exercise player

It should go without saying that a Design Team member can't be a player on the day of the exercise. They know everything about what's going to happen during the exercise, and it is usually very hard for them then to react to the narrative on exercise day as if they were learning about it for the first time. For smaller companies, this is challenging because the team of exercise players are small to begin with. If one of the most knowledge persons about a process or department must play in the exercise, find other ways to get the information you need from him or her. One way might be to schedule time to interview that person individually and ask a series of questions that go in a variety of directions but don't involve him/her in the Design Team meetings. This way, you can get a lot of information but, if you've asked wide-ranging questions, he.she really can't tell what scenario will used in the exercise.

How many Design Team members do you need?

Good question! The answer is that it isn't the number that counts. The better question is, "Do the people I have on the team cover all of the major areas to create the right injects and deliver the best experience?" So don't think about the number so much. Focus on the knowledge required for the narrative you have selected, and the experience you are trying to create. Having said that, a usual number is somewhere between five and ten.

For example, designing a cyber exercise will likely require Technology and Information Security Design Team members representing infrastructure, applications, database, networks and information security. However, your narrative may require others as well. On the Business Design Team, make sure that the key lines of business who will be impacted by the cyber breach are well represented. You will also likely need members who represent communications, government relations, investor relations, human resources, and others.

As you look at the list of likely Design Team members, consider if the people have a solid understanding of the business, technology, and information security environment to deliver the type of exercise experience you are looking for. If so, then you have the 'right' number of team members.

Design Team time commitment

It is always good to set expectations when soliciting Design Team members and to let them know how much time this will take. Here is a rough time estimate to consider:

- ▶ Attending all Design Team meetings: Usually 90 minutes to two hours each. There could be three-to-five of these depending on the length and complexity of the exercise.
- ▶ Completing homework assignments: Usually 30-minutes to one-hour per homework assignment for each meeting.

Why you need two design teams

EMSS has found the best success for a cyber scenario is to have two separate teams. A Technology Design Team should be very technical, detailed, and deeply in the weeds of the scenario. There should be a lot of time spent picking the right narrative and then dissecting it. The Technology Design Team should be identifying all the different affected systems and their interdependencies and connection points. Also, talk to them about how the scenario can be explained to the business design team who might not understand a highly technical discussion.

The Technology Design Team needs to do their work first, before the Business Unit Design Team begins, because you can't create the overall exercise injects until you know the technology issues and failures. Think of it like a Christmas tree – the IT issues, failures, and problems are the trunk and branches and provide the solid foundation for the story. The business unit injects are the reaction to those issues – like hanging ornaments on the tree. You can't hang the ornaments without the trunk and branches, you can't design the business unit injects, if you don't know the IT failures. (There is more about building the parallel narratives in Chapter 6.)

We always do the technology design first, followed by the business design, and then we circle back with the technology team to review the injects the business team has developed to make sure they align with the stated technology issues.

> *"Coming together is a beginning.*
> *Keeping together is progress.*
> *Working together is success."*
> —**Henry Ford**

Technology Design Team

For a cyber-based scenario, there are often five to eight members on the Technology Design Team. (Because of their experience in the company, some members can cover multiple topics.) You'll likely need subject matter experts in the following areas:

- ▶ Information Security
- ▶ Infrastructure
- ▶ Application Development & Support
- ▶ Network
- ▶ Database
- ▶ Network Operations Center
- ▶ Help Desk
- ▶ Storage

Business Unit Design Team

Your Business Unit Design Team has one primary goal – to develop the exercise injects that play off the cyber breach story. As mentioned, the BU Design Team shouldn't hold meetings until the Technology Design Team has completed its work. The type of members needed for your Business Unit team will depend on the overall cyber breach narrative. If you have a physical impact in the story as well as the cyber impact, you will also need to include facilities and security.

Business Unit Design Team members

A top-notch BU Design Team member will have several qualities:

- ▶ A good basic knowledge of the overall business.
- ▶ At least a year or more with the company in order to know some of the ins and outs of the place.
- ▶ Subject matter expertise in an area you will likely be touching

on in the narrative. A typical Design Team will include members from the following departments:
> Representatives from all of the key lines of business (to help you develop highly specific business injects).
> Facilities
> Physical Security
> Human Resources
> Communications
> Investor Relations

Note that the departments listed above are typical of Design Teams. Your organization may benefit from having team members representing a different 'slice' of your business.

The "other" role for your Design Team members to play

Design Team members usually make great Simulators. They know the exercise intimately and are already a cohesive team. If you plan to ask them to be Simulators in addition to their design job, in the interest of fair disclosure regarding the time commitment for the project, be sure to include that task when you ask for their participation. Additional time commitment for your Designer-turned-Simulator (approximate):

▶ Simulation Team orientation: Ninety-minutes to two-hours (usually a few days before the exercise).
▶ Exercise day: However long you have scheduled the exercise.

Design Team member checklist

Define the subject matter areas you need on the Design Team, brainstorm possible names, and then contact them (or their manager/supervisor) to secure their commitment to participate.

Technology Design

TECHNOLOGY DESIGN TEAM CHECKLIST			
ACTIVITY	NAME	EMAIL/PHONE #	COMMITMENT Y/N
Infrastructure			
Network			
Storage			
Database			
Application dev. & support			
Help desk			
Information security			
Network Ops Center			
Other area			
Other area			

Business Unit Design Team

BUSINESS UNIT DESIGN TEAM CHECKLIST			
SUBJECT MATTER AREA	NAME	EMAIL/PHONE #	COMMITMENT Y/N
Key departments or lines of business			
Facilities			
Security (physical)			
Human resources			
Communications			
Investor relations			
Other area			
Other area			
Other area			
Other area			

Design Team meetings

In my experience, most Design Team meetings last between 90-minutes and two-hours. They work equally well when held face-to-face or as a conference call. However, you might wish to do the first meeting face-to-face to make sure everyone is on point. I routinely hold Design Team meetings by conference call, and find them to be a highly efficient and effective use of everyone's time.

How many meetings to have and how often to have them

For an "average" cyber exercise, EMSS usually holds around four meetings for each team (eight total: four technology, four business). However, for a large functional or full-scale exercise you could easily do six to eight meetings for each team. It depends on the complexity, the length of the exercise, and the sophistication of the team.

Design Team meetings are usually held every other week. You don't want to lose the team's momentum by waiting too long between meetings. Conversely, the team needs time to do their homework (doing their 'trench coat' research or writing injects).

Who does what?

The Technology Design Team has two major tasks: develop the cyber breach narrative and develop the cyber breach injects. The Business Unit team develops the injects that reflect the impact of the technology situation on the organization. Hopefully, both sets of team members will act as Simulators on the day of the exercise. (More about this in Chapter 10.)

Exercise Design Team meeting checklist

Use this checklist as a guide in setting up both of your Design Team meetings

EXERCISE DESIGN TEAM MEETING CHECKLIST

PRIOR TO THE FIRST MEETING

- ☐ Develop a list of meeting dates and send out calendar notices for all.
- ☐ Secure a conference phone bridge or conference room for the meetings.
- ☐ Issue meeting invitations. Follow up with any team member who declines the meeting.
- ☐ Finalize the draft exercise goals and objectives.
- ☐ For the Business Design Team only: Have the full cyber narrative developed before the first meeting.

FIRST MEETING

- ☐ Give an orientation to exercises and exercise design:
    - ▷ Assign a due date for the homework. Issue the first homework assignment *(see next section)* **AND** assign a due date for the homework (This is very important; a task with no due date seldom, if ever, will be completed when you want it done.). Confirm details regarding to whom the homework will be returned and specifics regarding format, file naming conventions, and the like.
- ☐ Reaffirm the next Design Team meeting date.
- ☐ Check in with team members every two or three days to see if they are making progress or have any questions.

SUBSEQUENT MEETINGS

- ☐ Review the exercise plan:
    - ▷ Review any changes that have been made to the exercise plan.
    - ▷ Assure that the narrative still makes sense.
- ☐ Review all of the homework:
    - ▷ Go over each inject one by one.
    - ▷ Validate the information and the details of each inject.
    - ▷ Make sure the proposed caller isn't participating as a player in the exercise.
    - ▷ Verify you have enough injects for the length of exercise you are designing.
- ☐ Ask the question, "What are we missing?" Make sure the injects have adequately probed issuess concerning:
    - ▷ People – life safety concerns
    - ▷ Facilities issues
    - ▷ Technology
    - ▷ Communication
    - ▷ Time-sensitive activities that are at risk.
- ☐ Stand back and review where you are:
    - ▷ Assign homework as appropriate.
    - ▷ Set due date for the next homework assignment, if applicable.

EXERCISE DESIGN TEAM MEETING CHECKLIST
SUBSEQUENT MEETINGS
☐ Affirm the next meeting date. 　▷ If this is the last meeting: 　　> If there are still outstanding issues (insufficient number of injects, areas not completely explored), determine if you need to schedule another meeting to resolve them. If so, schedule the meeting. 　　> If the Design Team will be acting as the Simulation Team on the exercise day, confirm date and time of the Simulation Team training and the exercise.

Alone we can do so little, together we can do so much.

—Helen Keller

Summary

Both Design Teams are critical to a successful exercise. Selecting the right team members will make your exercise credible, exact, and challenging. It will also engage more people in your program and help to build a culture of awareness and support for your program.

CHAPTER SIX

The starting point: The exercise plan

Chapter goals:
1. Determine all of the components of a solid exercise plan.
2. Develop the scope, goals, and objectives of the exercise.
3. Appreciate the qualities of a "SMART" objective.
4. Learn to craft exercise artificialities and assumptions that contribute to the story.

An important document

The exercise plan lays out a fair amount of information for the exercise participants to know on exercise day. This chapter addresses most of the sections you should address in your exercise plan. Chapter Seven will talk about the narrative of the exercise separately.

The exercise plan should contain the following information:
- Exercise type
- Exercise scope
- Exercise goal(s)
- Exercise objectives
- Agenda
- Participant instructions
- Communications
- Evaluation
- Artificialities
- Assumptions

Exercise type

As discussed in Chapter Four, there are three types of exercises that best deliver the cyber narrative and experience to the players. By now, you should

have decided which one to create:
- Advanced Tabletop
- Functional
- Full-scale

Exercise scope

The scope of the exercise quickly tells the reader who is participating in the exercise and who is not. The exercise scope could consist of, but is not limited to, the following:
- Incident (Crisis) Management Team
- Senior executives (the "C" suite)
- Department Operations Centers (DOCs)[18]
- Technology
- Information Security
- Joint Information Center (JIC)[19]
- Key business units
- Other sites or critical locations

Defining the type and the scope of the exercise helps determine your physical and staffing requirements for the exercise. This includes the type of space and the number of Simulators and Observers that are needed.

Exercise goal

The exercise goal is the defined purpose of the exercise – answering my favorite question *"Why are we doing this exercise?" (see Chapter Seven)*. It keeps you on track to achieve the results you are seeking out of the experience.

Goals are developed by discovering what the key business leaders want to get out of the exercise experience through a series of interviews or conversations. For a cyber exercise, I normally like to chat with the following people to develop the exercise goal and objectives:
- Incident Commander

---

18 Department Operations Centers (DOCs) are often created for "first responder" departments. These "first responder" departments are often Physical Security, Facilities, IT, and Information Security. Occasionally, large business units will have them as well. Think of DOCs as "mini-command centers" that plug into the company's Incident Management Team.

19 A Joint Information Center (JIC) is a central location where personnel with *public information* responsibilities perform critical emergency information functions, crisis communications, and public affairs functions

- Business continuity manager
- Key business unit manager
- Key executives
- Technology and Information Security managers

It doesn't take a lot of questions to find out what people want to get out of the exercise; in fact, many times, I only need to ask one or two questions to learn everything I need. Here is my short list:

- What are you looking to achieve in this cyber exercise?
- Have you had any recent cyber incidents or Information Security activations? If yes, please tell me about them.
- How would you evaluate the overall cyber readiness of the organization?
- What are your top priorities, particularly with regard to threats the organization faces?

> *A goal without a plan is just a wish.*
> — *Antoine de Saint-Exupéry*

Exercise objectives

Exercise objectives are essentially sub-goals. They identify short-term, measurable steps that are moving toward achieving the overall exercise goal. I develop exercise objectives in two ways:

- During the initial interviews, I pay close attention to the answer to the "what do you want to get out of the exercise?" question. This one identifies what is important and where there are likely to be issues to explore.
- I go back to the basic question, *Why are you doing this exercise?* It sheds light on the exercise objectives and gives a wealth of information.

The many benefits of exercise objectives

Objectives are like touchstones, going back to them again and again through the entire design process. It is important to spend the time to develop and validate them.

- ▶ Guide the design
  - > Objectives are used to guide the design in the beginning and to assess the outcome at the end. Well-written objectives will sharpen and narrow the scope of the exercise plan. Does the narrative meet all of your expected outcomes? Go back and look at the objectives. When you want to make sure you are still on track, go back to the objectives. When you are trying to assess whether or not you have a complete set of injects, go back to the objectives. They are the guiding light of the design process.
- ▶ Provide direction for the exercise narrative
  - > Objectives set the direction of the exercise. Well-written objectives will always point to the best narrative to achieve them. Objectives also help to keep the exercise and the players on track.
- ▶ Frame exercise injects
  - > The objectives control the direction and type of exercise injects. For example, if one of your objectives is about communications (employee, client, media, etc.), then you will likely have several injects that will raise communication issues from those entities.
- ▶ Provide context to evaluate the exercise
  - > Lastly, objectives are used to evaluate the exercise. When assessing the exercise, look to the objectives to assure each of them was achieved.

Objectives: Are six too many? Are two enough?

There is no set number of objectives that an exercise should have. Ideally, there should be the number necessary to address the issues you are trying to raise and assess in the exercise. Most cyber exercises will have between 5 to 10 objectives. There may also be additional sub-objectives for a specific team, a department, or location.

Characteristics of good objectives

Writing good objectives takes a bit of practice. Objectives should be clear

and easily understandable. A well-written objective should be:
- ▶ Simple
- ▶ Concise
- ▶ Measurable (when possible)
- ▶ Achievable
- ▶ Realistic and challenging

A strong objective details what is expected from the player and if they are able to demonstrate that he or she can perform the skill or task. In particular, well-written objectives use strong "action verbs" to describe that behavior. Action verbs are those that specifically describe what the subject of the objective is doing. They are observable and better communicate the intent of what is to be completed.

SMART objectives

"SMART" is an acronym to assist you in writing strong objectives.[20] It is a catchy little word that touches on the specific qualities of well-written objectives. The objectives should be:
- ▶ **S**pecific – Explicit, with a key result. It should be clear about what, where, when, and how the situation will be changed.
- ▶ **M**easurable – Clear as to whether you are meeting the objective or not, and quantify the targets and benefits.
- ▶ **A**chievable – Attainable.
- ▶ **R**ealistic – Practical enough to be met, especially within the confines of an exercise time limit.
- ▶ **T**ime bound – A defined time period in which the objective will be accomplished.

Exercise agenda

Don't forget to "plan out" your time for the exercise day. You may be estimating that your exercise "playtime" will be for 2 to 4 hours, but your exercise participants will be with you longer than that. ("Playtime" is the time the participants will be actively engaged in the narrative.) Develop an agenda

---

20 I found no one clear author for the concept although it is found in *Leadership and the One Minute Manager: Increasing Effectiveness Through Situational Leadership*, Ken Blanchard, Patricia Zigarmi, Drea Zigarmi, William Morrow, 1999.

and socialize it to make sure all players know what the time commitment will be. (You may want to review some of the sample agendas in Chapter Four.)

Exercise duration

Talking about an agenda naturally leads to another fairly basic question: how long should the actual exercise playtime be? Your exercise can be a half- or full-day format, but that time usually includes introductions, plan review, debriefings, and other "non-play" activities. In terms of actual playtime, you will need to determine how long the players should be "playing" before there is a break/meal or a change in the story (such as advancing the exercise time clock).

To do justice to a cyber narrative, EMSS recommends at least three hours of play time to fully explore the issues, the impacts, and address the strategic policy questions that are sure to surface. Our exercises usually run anywhere from three to six hours, and we do not advance the clock in the narrative. It is too complicated to advance the clock – it requires a very detailed narrative about what happened in-between the time elements, it can be very confusing for players and it is hard to second guess decisions that the exercise players could make.

> *Plans are nothing; planning is everything.*
> *— Dwight D. Eisenhower*

Participant instructions

This section of the exercise plan tells the exercise players what they can expect from the exercise and what is expected of them during the exercise. It really gives you, the designer, a chance to communicate your thoughts and intentions and introduce what might be some new concepts to the players.

"Stay in role"

One important concept to communicate in the instructions is the expectation that the players will "stay in role" during the exercise play time. That simply means they shouldn't be talking about what they did last weekend or the television show they watched last night. They need to be in the here and now, to act and believe that this incident is really happening. When done this way, after a short period of time, the mind can't tell the difference between what is real and what is imagined. If they start talking about how bad it would be if this "were to happen," it's your job to remind them that it has![21]

Expect mistakes

Problems, issues, and mistakes in an exercise are a good thing. An overarching goal of any exercise is to find out what doesn't work. Some people are very concerned about their performance and about making mistakes. A cyber scenario in particular can have many hidden political 'landmines' due to the sensitive nature of the topic. You need to reassure the players that making mistakes is inherently part of the learning process. Exercises are not a "fault-finding activity." There is no grade issued at the end of the experience. There will likely be a lot of mistakes – and that is a good thing.

Embrace "Exercise Magic"

I created the term "exercise magic" some years ago to explain some of the exercise creativity we use in the narrative, the story, the scene, and the experience. For example, how did this team just "magically" come together? How is it that you learned about this narrative as you did? Whatever their question is, I ask players to not get hung up in how things have happened. We have simply used a bit of "exercise magic" to create this event. If we somehow missed the mark, don't get hung up, don't fight the narrative, and please don't say "This could never happen." We ask the players not to debate that something has happened, could have happened, or is happening – just accept that it is!

"Time-outs"

There is occasionally a need to take a "time out." There are two primary reasons:.
1. ***A real emergency happens.*** It is important that you let everyone know what you will do if a real emergency happens in the middle of the exercise –

---

[21] "Imagination Can Change Perceptions of Reality," Psychology Today, Christopher Bergland, June 28, 2013

obviously, the exercise stops and the incident is assessed and managed. If it is a small issue, such as a false fire alarm, you may be able to get back to your exercise. If it's a bona fide emergency, then the team gets to "practice" for real.

2. ***The team is so off track that you can't "right them" any other way.*** In my many years, I have only had this happen once. The team had so wrapped themselves around a proverbial axle that the only way to unwrap them was to announce a "time out" and set the record straight. Better to do that than to have them off-base the entire time.

Don't be afraid to use a "time out" if that is what it would take to get the exercise back on track. The simplest way to do a time out is to simply stand in the middle of the exercise space/room and with a loud outdoor voice call out to everyone, "Excuse, me; excuse me. I need to make an announcement." Then simply correct whatever issue needs to be corrected or state whatever needs to be stated. Once you are done, thank them and tell them, "the exercise is now resuming – carry on!"

Communications

The communications section of the exercise plan tells the players everything they need to know about exercise communication. This section details:
- ▶ Who is appropriate for them to communicate with and who it is not.
- ▶ What your expectations are for communications. In an Advanced Tabletop, Functional, or Full-scale exercise, players should simulate all communications that they would do in a real incident using the Simulation Team or whomever else you allow them to call.
- ▶ Describe who the Simulation Team is and how to use them.
- ▶ In a Functional or Full-scale exercise, injects will be delivered using phones, so you will need to detail how to use the exercise phone directory.

Evaluation

The evaluation section should discuss how the exercise will be evaluated. In this short section, you simply state the different methods you are using to evaluate the exercise. We usually use a combination of participant evaluations, observer comments, and the facilitator's observations.

Artificialities

The artificialities section will describe all of the things that are blatantly "pretend" for the exercise, and are obviously not true. You can think oft the exercise artificialities as things that would improve your exercise if you could simply change them. There are three examples that might be helpful for you to consider:
- ▶ Changes to date and/or time
- ▶ People who are unavailable
- ▶ Conditions necessary to conduct the exercise

This is one of the great things about an exercise – you can do anything you like. You are creating the reality that your players will have to operate in. You can be king or queen of your exercise world!

Changes to date and/or time

The date or time is one of the most common things to modify. During your design process, explore which dates and times might have a great impact on the organization. A "great impact" in our minds, is one that creates more challenges for the players. Make the decision to declare the scenario date as a different date from the actual exercise date if it makes sense for the maturation of the team. Some examples:
- ▶ If having this cyber exercise during a heavy processing period would make it much more challenging for the business, it might be a good idea to move the date to one that is smack dab in the middle of, for example, month-, quarter-, or year-end challenges.
- ▶ If (for example) the trading desk closes at noon, but your exercise begins at 1:00 PM, consider changing the exercise time to 9:00 or 10:00 AM to create an added sense of urgency in the players.

Unavailable people

One of the great fallacies of a response situation is believing that all of your staff will be able to show up after any crisis. I hear this from clients all the time: "Oh yes, everyone here is dedicated and will do whatever they can to get to work to help recover the business." But what if they are on vacation in Bali or hiking in the Sierras? And what if that person was your most knowledgeable IT person? Thanks to a well-chosen artificiality, that key person could be unavailable, forcing the players to figure out how to handle a real-life situation.

Assumptions

It is human nature to make assumptions when faced with missing or incomplete facts. To avoid having your exercise participants doing this on their own (and probably creating facts that are not what you wanted or expected in the process), clearly state any assumptions that apply to the exercise narrative. You should also state that any questions or clarifications should be directed to the facilitator — that participants are not allowed to answer their own questions.

When you clearly lay out the ground rules and tell people what they can assume (and sometimes what they can't assume), you are less likely to have conflict in the course of the exercise.

> *If you don't know where you are going, you'll end up someplace else."*
> — *Yogi Berra*

Sample exercise plan

The following is a sample of an exercise plan for an advanced tabletop exercise.

1. Exercise type and scope
- Advanced tabletop exercise
- Incident involving the activation of the Senior Leadership Team

2. Exercise goal
- To challenge the Senior Leadership Team to manage a cyber incident and develop appropriate responses

3. Exercise agenda

ADVANCED TABLETOP EXERCISE AGENDA		
ACTIVITY	**TIME**	**DISCUSSION LEADER**
Introduction and review of exercise logistics	8:00 AM – 8:15 AM	Facilitator
Advanced tabletop exercise	8:15 AM – 11:30 AM	Facilitator
Short break to grab lunch	11:30-11:45	
Debrief over lunch	11:45 AM – 12:45 PM	Facilitator
Next steps	12:45 PM – 1:00 PM	Business Continuity Manager

4. Exercise objectives
1. Demonstrate the team's ability to conduct an initial assessment.
2. Evaluate the ability of the team to develop an incident action plan in a timely manner.
3. Confirm senior leadership's ability to select an effective media spokesperson.
4. Prove that the communications team is prepared to handle media challenges.
5. Assess the timeliness and accuracy of the communications messaging.
6. Evaluate a cyber incident strategy developed by the Senior Leadership Team.

5. Instructions to participants
- ▶ Exercises have the greatest value if they are treated as real. Stay in role the entire time.
- ▶ In order to make this exercise work and to facilitate the learning process, a certain amount of "exercise magic" has been used. We ask you not to debate that something has happened, could have happened, or is available – it just is!
- ▶ Don't just think about responding to what is coming at you – remember to keep one eye into the future and play the game of "what-if."
- ▶ Please do not make up an answer to respond to a query or inject. You need to communicate with the Simulation Team. If you need a piece of "real" information, you may contact a "real" company department. Just tell them you are in an exercise and you need a piece of information and then conclude the call.
- ▶ As the exercise progresses, details may not be as complete as you would like. The value is in the process, the dialogue, and the experience. The Design Team has worked to make the situations as realistic as possible.
- ▶ You may only use what is in place as of today; if new equipment is being added next month, it is not in place and can't be used.
- ▶ Exercises are for learning; we expect mistakes. The goal is to develop the team and learn from the experience. There is no "pass" or "fail" in this exercise. It is

expected that many mistakes will be made – an exercise is a valuable learning experience to see if the plans that were developed are sufficient.
- Questions regarding the exercise should be directed to the exercise facilitator.

6. Exercise control
- Periodic pre-scripted messages will be used throughout this exercise.
- An exercise facilitator will monitor the exercise and adjust the flow of messages to provide the maximum training benefit for the participants.

7. Communications
- A Simulation Team will act as the "outside world" for this exercise. All problems must be solved by "calling" the Sim Team, acting as proxies for the outside world.
- If you need a piece of "real" information, you may contact a "real" company department. Just tell them you are in an exercise and you need a piece of information and then conclude the call.
- All information in the narrative and that provided by the facilitator is to be considered valid. However, just like in a real disaster, messages can be jumbled, and rumors can start on incorrect information or assumptions. Multiple versions of the same situation may occur.

8. Evaluation
The exercise will be evaluated by use of participant written evaluations, the debrief session, and evaluators' observations based on the objectives.

9. Exercise assumptions
- All information in the narrative is to be considered valid.
- All information provided by the facilitator is to be considered valid.
- Don't assume anything else. All information can be verified by asking the facilitator(s).
- You may wonder how these calls and other questions will be coming to you at your location during this emergency. This is part of "exercise magic" – just go with it.
- None of the Senior Leadership Team members were impacted by this incident.
- Everyone is able to participate.

10. Exercise artificialities
- The time is the real time.
- The stock market has been quite volatile the past few days with the market going up and down 200 – 400 points per day.
- You team has been called together to discuss a possible threat.

11. Exercise narrative
The narrative will be revealed to you during the course of the exercise.

Summary

The Exercise Plan is the foundation for the exercise experience. With the exception of the artificialities and assumptions (which will be developed along with the narrative), the plan document should be constructed and approved before the first Design Team meeting. Look at this critical document as a road map, with all of the rules of the road carefully laid out for the design team and exercise players to review – and agree to – before the exercise begins.

CHAPTER SEVEN

What drives the story? The narrative

Chapter goals:
1. Learn the power of "the silly question."
2. Know how to guide the Technology Design team to develop the technology failures that drive the exercise.
3. Understand how to craft exercise artificialities, assumptions, and the two narratives.
4. See how to weave the business and technology narrative together into an impactful story and experience.
5. Assess the need for one or more "physical" impacts to engage all of your exercise players.

The "Silly Question"

There is one question you want to ask yourself, your colleagues, your Design Team, and others over and over again during the design process. This question will help you stay on track and on vision from start to finish: *"Why are we doing this exercise?"* Don't be turned off by the simplicity of that question, the answer holds the key to your exercise.

I started asking this "silly question" when I noticed how easy it was for people to get caught up in the excitement of the design. The team would be so fully engaged in the process that there were suddenly Martians landing in the middle of the exercise (metaphorically, of course), and things were being added to the exercise that didn't support the goals or objectives. This is really easy to do in a cyber exercise. Be alert, and keep asking Why are we doing this exercise? to avoid filling your exercise with things that don't align with your objectives and can end up derailing the experience.

When embarking on the design process, this "silly question" can help you and the Design Team stay on track and deliver the type of exercise you want.

> *There's always room for a story
> that can transport people to another place.*
> — *J. K. Rowlng*

Narrative development

The exercise narrative for a cyber scenario is designed by two different Design Teams: a Technology Design Team and a Business Design Team. This will, of course, extend the length of the design time and will likely increase the number of Design Team participants. This chapter peels back the development of these parallel narratives.

Technology narrative

As discussed in Chapter 3, you must have a willing IT/Information Security Department to have a successful cyber exercise. During the narrative design stage is when their true willingness is put to the test; discussing a possible hacking incident and the subsequent failures can give your IT Department the willies. When you have this first discussion with them, it's a bit like leading them down the path of lots of small 'yesses' to finally get to the big 'yes' and into the real hacking discussion. In our exercise experiences, it goes something like this:

- Ask the Technology Design Team the first hard question: "Could our company be hacked?" This often causes a bit of nervous laughter, a bit of shifting in the chairs, a bit of looking down at the table. Spend a few minutes reassuring them that it's okay to be honest, but you need to know, truthfully – could the company be hacked?
- Of course, as you might guess, the answer is always yes. Getting this first 'yes' is the most important one and often makes people feel very uncomfortable. They fear they might be perceived as not doing their job, they might be blamed--- the "I could get fired" fear.
- The next question to ask is, "How could that happen?" At that point (usually), the conversation starts to blossom and the real exchange begins. Here are some great examples – intrusion vehicles – of how it can happen[22]:

---

22 "Ways Companies Get Hacked" http://www.cnbc.com/2012/07/06/10-Ways-Companies-Get-Hacked.html

CYBER BREACH 59

- Rogue employee (insider threat)
- Foreign nation players
- Spear phishing
- "Drive-by" web-download
- USB key malware
- Servers being scanned for vulnerabilities
- Users tricked into sharing their passwords
- Wi-Fi compromises
- Stolen credentials from a third party
- Compromising web-based databases
- Exploiting password reset services

Ultimately, though, the biggest reason for a breach is employees…humans…us! You can redesign software and tighten up systems but humans – all of us – remain the weakest link. A quote from *Fast Company* magazine and security blogger Graham Cluley is so true: "Humans can't be upgraded. You can't fix the bug in people's brain that makes them click a link, or choose a really dumb password."[23]

(As a side note, for your exercise scenario, all you need to know is that a breach is possible. The IT/Information Security Department needs to identify a way it could happen, but during the course of the exercise, the participants will never really know exactly how they were hacked. It takes weeks and sometimes months for the forensics of a breach to be completed. An amazing 2014 study of U.K. companies revealed that 81% of them had suffered malicious data breaches and one-in-five didn't even know it.[24] So for this exercise, all the players need to know is that it is possible.)

Once IT has identified the intrusion vehicle, there are a few more decisions that need to be made:

▶ How long ago did the intrusion occur? The exercise players will never know how far back the hack goes, but the Business Design Team needs to know so they can reflect that in their injects. In EMSS exercises, we

---

23 "Why do companies keep getting hacked?" Fast Company http://www.fastcompany.com/3026672/the-code-war/why-do-companies-keep-getting-hacked
he last portion is ave been hacked. Guardian e a malware ompleted. hacked - that ar of not doing their job, fear of being blame

24 "How to tell if you have been hacked". Guardian March 23, 2015 http://www.theguardian.com/technology/2015/mar/23/how-to-tell-if-youve-been-hacked

go back at least 30 days; in some cases, our scenario has gone back a full year. This gives you more options for Bad Things to happen. The terminology we use is "T-minus" (days, hours, or minutes). You might be familiar with this terminology from NASA rocket launches. (And in case you are curious, the "T" doesn't stand for 'time,' but rather 'test'.[25])

▶ How will the "hack" be revealed? How is it discovered? For your purposes, it could be because the hacker "went public" or it could be because of the way systems "melt down." It could be something obvious like the Sony compromise when the attackers changed the computer screens to proclaim the hack[26], or it could be more insidious where users experience missing files and error messages that increase over time.

Now that you've identified this critical baseline information, it's time to begin the design in earnest.

Technology narrative phases

EMSS has found that by dividing the narrative into phases within the exercise is a helpful way to stay on track, not melt down the systems too quickly, and keep the injects better organized. Think of it like the well-known (but incorrect) urban legend of boiling a frog: Place a frog in cool water and then turn up the heat so it cooks before it knows it. While contemporary biologists say that the premise of the story is false (a frog submerged and gradually heated will jump out), it is still a good way to view this exercise design.[27]

An example of the different phases might look something like this:

Phase one

An initial threat inject starts off the exercise story. At this point, everything is highly speculative: Could this have really happened? Is this person really in our systems? Could they do that? The team can discuss how serious the threat might be and whether or not it is real. As part of this initial conversation, the team will learn (via injects) about the other minor things that hap-

---

25 https://www.quora.com/"Why-do-they-say-T-Minus-while-counting-down-for-the-launch-of-rocket."
26 "Sony, The Hack of the Century", Fortune Magazine, http://fortune.com/sony-hack-part-1/
27 "Boiling Frogs", Wikipedia, https://en.wikipedia.org/wiki/Boiling_frog

pened the previous day or week, which will make them wonder further if a breach is real and if the issues they are hearing about are tied to the threat. The goal of Phase One is to have the players discuss the issues, possibilities, and "what ifs." Again, at this point, everything is all quite uncertain.

Phase two

In this phase, the issues become a increasingly difficult and all decisions have major implications for the business. The perpetrator reveals a video they sent to the company that clearly states they aren't kidding and "things" are going to start happening to the company "soon, very soon." The tone is threatening, but not sinister.

Also in this phase, it's time to kick up the pain for the employees: the network is slow, attempts to reach the customer-facing website are misdirected to an offensive site, and other seemingly trivial events get reported. Injects presented in this phase are designed to get the team to consider whether they should isolate the network from the internet. Is this hack real?

Phase three

In Phase Three, the tension really starts to build. In Phase Two, the perpetrator sent a video to the company, but in Phase Three, the perpetrator "outs" the hack to the news media and their Twitter page, as well as to the company's Twitter and Facebook pages. The players experience injects that show an increase in the number of error messages, incorrect files, and other anomalies. The network is getting slower and slower, and more and more employees are complaining. The customer call center is being inundated with problems regarding errors that customers are finding on their accounts.

Injects that are presented in Phase Three are designed to make the team ask if they should isolate the company – disconnect from the Internet or cut the core network.

"The purpose of a storyteller
is not to tell you how to think,
but to give you questions to think upon."
*~ **Brandon Sanderson**, The Way of Kings*

First Technology Design Team meeting agenda

Here is what a typical first technology Design Team meeting might look like:

- ▶ Introduction
- ▶ Discuss goals and objectives
- ▶ Review the exercise players (so the team can imagine who will be interacting with the material
- ▶ Discuss the possibility and probability of being hacked
- ▶ Brainstorm the penetration effects or impacts
- ▶ Assign homework and announce next meeting date

TECHNOLOGY TIMELINE DOCUMENT		
TIME	**TARGET**	**EFFECT**
T+ 0:20		Users reporting that files are missing.
T+0:30	Website	Call center is receiving calls that customers are being redirected to an "offensive" company website (such as a porn site) when they attempt to log into their account.
T+0:45	Active Directory	Replication failures are occurring.
T+0:55	Application	Users cannot access SAP, getting many error messages.
T+1:10	MWare vCenter	MWare admins cannot log into VMWare Center anymore. It appears to time out.
T+1:20	Windows Print	User print jobs are continuously failing.
T+1:30	Windows	Users attempting to log in take upwards of 5 minutes to reach the log-in prompt and a further 5-10 minutes to log in.
T+1:40	Active Directory	<<Server Name>>, a key server, is unavailable.
T+1:50	Network	Internal network performance is degraded, everything is slow.
T+2:00		User reports that his H" drive appears empty.
T+2:10	Print	Print jobs seem to work for only 1 out of every 10 users.

And so on. More bad wews continues to be delivered as the systems melt down.

The technology timeline document will become the backbone of the exercise and the narrative. It must be developed and *fully* vetted by the Technology

Design Team. *It should have as much detail as is necessary to tell the story, develop the injects and the experience, and be credible.* This will take several meetings and homework assignments between each meeting.

Subsequent Technology Design Team meeting agenda

Remaining Technology Design Team meeting agendas could look like this:

- Revisit the goals and objectives. Are the failures meeting our objectives?
- Review the current status of the technology timeline.
- What is missing and needs to be added?
- What is extraneous?
- Continue to brainstorm the hack effects or impacts.
- he last portion is ave been hacked. Guardian e a malware ompleted. hacked - that ar of not doing their job, fear of being blame
- Assign homework and announce next meeting date.

In the final meeting, the technology narrative needs to be explicitly announced as being 'done.' No future tweaking can occur, as it will then get turned over to the Business Design Team, which will be developing their injects based on the technology scenario. Mucking about with the technology story and timeline after the business team has started their work has the potential to completely derail the business unit injects, which must "dance" with the technology narrative.

The Technology Design Team then gets a well-deserved break as the Business Unit Design Team kicks into gear.

Business narrative

The business narrative is the story of how the technology failures affect the business side. Since the participants can't go to a computer to see these technology failures, the business injects tell the exercise player what is going on. (The development of these injects will be discussed in Chapter 8.)

Physical impact

One of your jobs as an exercise designer is to engage all of the players. If

you are designing this exercise for a "typical" incident management or crisis management team, you may need to come up with an event for this exercise that has a physical component in order to engage *all* of the players. Typically, the Facilities and Physical Security teams won't have much to do in a cyber exercise. If you need to engage them in your exercise, there are several different ways you can do that:
- A technological way to engage those teams is to have the hacker "play" with the electronic systems that control the building:
  > The Building Management System that controls the HVAC, water coolers, towers, or other building equipment is causing the heat to come on in summer or air conditioning to come in winter.
  > The fire alarm system is compromised and the fire alarms are going off at different time even though there are no fires.
  > The access management system is disabled and everything opens and can't be shut, or everything closes and can't be opened.
- If a technological hack of the building systems isn't possible, some other physical impact needs to be introduced so Facilities and Physical Security (and other groups) will be engaged in the exercise. After all, the real world will continue to turn as your hacking story unfolds. Other events that EMSS has used to get all the players involved have included:
- Protracted power outage (building, utility)
  > Construction accident in the immediate area
  > Explosion at a steam plan causing loss of heat in winter
  > Fire in a critical location of the building
  > Infrastructure failure, such as a water pipe break, that shorts out an electrical panel

> *"No, no! The adventures first,*
> *explanations take such a dreadful time."*
> — ***Lewis Carroll***
> *Alice's Adventures in Wonderland & Through the Looking-Glass*

Summary

The technology narrative is critical. Take your time with your Technology Design Team to select a narrative that will best meet your objectives and deliver the experience you are aiming to give the players. And then keep it very close to your vest. You don't want the players to figure out things in advance.

CHAPTER EIGHT

Moving the exercise forward – Exercise injects

Chapter goals:
1. Learn what exercise injects are.
2. See why you need them.
3. Identify the purpose and characteristics of an inject.
4. Understand different methods for inject delivery.

What are exercise injects?

In an exercise, you start with a baseline narrative, but exercise injects get move the story forward.

An inject is simply a pre-scripted message that is provided to players during the course of an exercise. It can be provided to the exercise players using a variety of methods (see "Exercise Inject Delivery Methods" below). Injects continue the story that began with the baseline narrative you gave the team at the start of the exercise.

Remember, in an exercise, you are creating an entire world of make believe. You are creating the story, the movie, or the television show, and in the narrative of the exercise plan, you've only told the players how it begins. If you don't tell them something has changed or the situation has progressed, how else would they know? Injects move the story from the baseline narrative. They make the exercise come alive.

> *If you don't tell them, they don't know.*
> — *Regina Phelps*

What Is the purpose of an exercise inject?

In addition to providing more information about how the story is progressing, most exercise injects are meant to ask the recipient **to do something.** After all, the exercise is about working towards the exercise objectives and, ultimately, achieving the goal of the exercise. This requires the players to respond, to act, or to do something. Therefore, most injects will have one or more questions to be answered or issues to be resolved. It is possible for some injects to simply provide additional background information regarding the storyline. Or they may act as additional data or "FYI" to the players relating to an issue or situation. These informational injects should be a very small percentage (less than 5%) of your total injects.

Other than purely "FYI" injects, the other injects should trigger action among the participants in at least one of four ways:
Gather,
Decide,
Collaborate or
Defer.

Gather

Injects may require players to gather information, and confer with other players to solve the problem.

Decide

Exercises are an action-oriented activity. Many injects will likely require the players to make a decision about something they need do to manage the incident.

Collaborate

Sometimes an inject will require players to discuss, deliberate, and/or consult with others. These could be people inside their own team, on other teams, or perhaps the Simulation Team. A well-framed inject is a great way to determine (or illuminate) interdependencies. They also ensure that you have identified the right players for the team.

Defer

Not everything is critical. Not everything requires immediate action. If you only gave someone one inject, it's possible they could work on that one inject all day long. What if they had to handle two, three, four, or more injects? At some point, they would have to prioritize what they need to do, and decide which ones are simply not important enough and are deferrable. Often giving them lower-level issues or low-priority problems to handle is a good training tool, as humans have a tendency to work on everything that is presented to them. Providing some issues that don't need immediate attention helps players learn how to establish priorities in a high pressure situation.

> *There are two ways to share knowledge:*
> *You can **push** information out*
> *or you can **pull** them in with a story.*
> *— Anonymous*

Exercise inject characteristics

Exercise injects move the exercise forward and have several qualities:
- ▶ Point to the objectives
- ▶ Describe a situation – critically important in a cyber incident
- ▶ Stimulate the player to do something
- ▶ Escalate an issue

Point to the Objectives

Injects generally point toward the objectives. This goes back to the discussion on exercise objectives (Chapter 6) and how important they are. As you design the injects, your eye should always be on the objectives. What are you trying to achieve in this exercise?

For example, if you have an objective regarding communications (i.e., developing media, customer or employee communications), you need injects that require that type of response. This means you will likely have injects with queries from the media, customers, and employees – all of which require some type of communication response.

Describe a situation

After the baseline narrative has been reviewed at the start of the exercise, how do the players know that anything has happened or that there has been a change to the story? This type of inject is critical in a cyber incident, as the players can't go to a computer to see what is happening. They need to be told what's happening via the injects. Injects will tell the story of the technology failures through issues related to – for example – an inability to access systems, perform business processes, access websites, or use VOIP. The injects paint the picture.

Stimulate action

As previously described, the overriding priority of most injects is action. The goal of an inject is to stimulate the participants to action – to get them to do something.

An inject can also escalate an initial or primary problem from the narrative and create secondary or tertiary problems. For example, in a malware scenario, consider the following:

- ▶ *Primary event:* A technology failure, such as data corruption or missing files, is described at the beginning of the exercise.
- ▶ *Secondary event:* As the exercise progresses, critical files regarding private client information are released by the perpetrator creating significant brand damage.
- ▶ *Tertiary event:* The news media pick up on the breach and loss of sensitive data, and now the company's reputation is severely damaged.

Your job as the designer is to plot out this storyline escalation strategy and have a clear vision of where the exercise is going so the injects support that vision.

Exercise inject delivery methods

There are several ways to inject information into an exercise. The only thing that may limit the choices is your imagination – and perhaps your budget. The following methods are most often used:

- ▶ Message Center forms (later in this chapter)
- ▶ Phone
- ▶ Fax

- Email
- Mock broadcast, radio, or video (from a local station or entity such as CNN)
- Mock FBI report (reporting your hack)
- Mock newspaper article (from a local newspaper)
- Mock website story (from news sites such as Reuters or NYTimes, or from a post on a social media site such as Facebook or Twitter)
- Actor playing a role

The best delivery method

The "best" delivery method will depend on your team and situation. An exercise that employs several methods of inject delivery is, of course, both more interesting and challenging.

Information sources

Information will come into your exercise from a variety of sources – some that you can control (like injects), and others that you can't. It is important to recognize these multiple sources and be aware of them. One of these sources could possibly start to derail your exercise, and you need to know how to identify it, and then – if needed – "right" the exercise to keep it on track. Be aware of information that makes its way to your players from the following sources: injects, "making stuff up" and player assumptions and ad hoc information.

The pre-scripted injects that your Design Team has worked so hard to create are the things that you know about and can control. They should contain the information you want and need the players to receive.

"Making stuff up" and player assumptions

Exercise players have been known to start "making stuff up" as the exercise goes along. You, of course, can't control their minds, but you need to be aware that they're doing it, and know what it is they're making up. Your own observations and the observations of the evaluators and controllers can help you keep an eye on this as the exercise moves along. This can also occur when the players start inserting their unverified assumptions into the exercise.

Ad hoc information

Simulators or the facilitator/controllers may present spontaneous information as the exercise progresses. This is likely to occur for the following reasons:

- ▶ **Push a particular issue.** The players might not be "getting" or understanding an important issue in the exercise, You need to interject more or different information into the exercise to push the issue.
- ▶ **Right a misconception.** Along the way, an assumption may have been made that needs correcting. This can be done by delivering an ad hoc inject to right the story.
- ▶ **Combat some made-up player information.** As discussed above, players will sometimes make up their own information; occasionally, their made-up stories or assumptions will directly conflict with the exercise design.
- ▶ **Correct the direction the exercise is taking.** Players might have come up with an idea or assumption that is in direct conflict with your design, either due to their own agenda or because the issue wasn't clearly addressed in the design. If an assumption is being made that is going to create havoc with future injects and the story line, your Simulation Team needs to call in a spontaneous inject to correct that misconception.

The greatest art in the world is the art of storytelling.
— **Cecil B. DeMille**

Designing the business injects

Once the Technology narrative is done, the first Business Unit Design Team meeting can be held. You will need a Technology Design Team member or two to be in attendance for the first meeting (and maybe more of them) to explain in plain language what all those technology failures mean.

First Business Unit Design Team meeting agenda

Here is what a typical first design team meeting might look like:
- ▶ Discuss goals and objectives

- ▶ Review the exercise players (so the team can imagine who will be interacting with the material)
- ▶ Take a deep dive on the cyber narrative in easy-to-understand language so that everyone can grasp how it will affect their business
- ▶ Brainstorm the effects or impacts of the hack
- ▶ Assign homework and announce next meeting date

Subsequent Business Unit Design Team meetings

Other Design Team meeting agendas may look like this:
- ▶ Revisit the goals and objectives to determine if the injects are meeting the objectives.
- ▶ Review the injects from the homework:
  - > Do any conflict with others?
  - > Do they make sense?
- ▶ Dig deeper:
  - > What is missing and needs to be added?
  - > What is extraneous and can be eliminated?
- ▶ Brainstorm the hack's effects or impacts.
- ▶ Assign homework and announce next meeting date.

Continue these meetings until you have met your objectives, demonstrated all of the technology failures, and created the number of injects that are needed. It is very helpful to have a list of the exercise players on hand and make sure that all players have some injects delivered to them so they are engaged in the exercise.

Sample Business Unit injects

A sample of what business injects might look like is on the next four pages. This is the typical form EMSS uses for exercises. Once the injects are finalized, the "Design Team Member" column is changed to the "Simulator" column and the name of the assigned Simulator is placed in the box. The "Routing" column is the exercise player name and/or department (the recipient) that will receive the inject during the exercise. For "Caller's Name," we always try to find real names of real people to make it feel like the real deal for the participants.

SAMPLE BUSINESS UNIT INJECTS

CALL #	TIME	DESIGN TEAM MEMBER (SIMULATOR)	ROUTING	CALLER'S NAME, TITLE & DEPT	CALL SCRIPT
1				<<Caller name, title, dept>>	My visitors from <<company name>> will be arriving in two hours and I need to do that video conference with them. Where can I go?
2				<<Caller name, title, dept>>	We have issues printing <<name of>> reports. Sometimes it prints and other times it does not. Can someone help us?
3				<<Caller name, title, dept>>	We posted our transactions into the Billing system however the data did not transfer to SAP, therefore, we can't balance our end-of-day.
4				<<Caller name, title, dept>>	We try to insert the <<name of>> reports into Sharepoint but cannot because we are unable to access <<app name>>. Is there an issue with Sharepoint?
5				<<Caller name, title, dept>>	I was outside the building on break and was approached by two representatives from the media requesting information. They heard that we have been hacked. They are asking me how bad it is. What do I tell them or who should I refer them too?
6				<<Caller name, title, dept>>	I cannot open the <<name of>> spreadsheet. I can't update my cash flows.
7				<<Caller name, title, dept>>	My workstation was identified as one of the ones that are compromised. Do I have to use another workstation? Where can I go to work?

CYBER BREACH   75

SAMPLE BUSINESS UNIT INJECTS

CALL #	TIME	DESIGN TEAM MEMBER (SIMULATOR)	ROUTING	CALLER'S NAME, TITLE & DEPT	CALL SCRIPT
8				<<Caller name, title, dept>>	There's a problem with Reuters. If not fixed, this will affect the quote sheet that we send our vendors and the closing foreign exchange rates.
9				<<Caller name, title, dept>>	I am trying to get into PeopleSoft to see how much vacation I have left because I need to take some time off next week. I keep getting error messages.
10				<<Caller name, title, dept>>	I am buying a new house and my bank needs to see a copy of my last pay statement, and I can't get it from the system. What can I do?
12				<<Caller name, title, dept>>	I was supposed to provide a briefing on an <<name of topic>> to our Board next week, and it is due today. I can't access my J drive to get it. What should I do?
13				<<Caller name, title, dept>>	We are starting to get a lot of calls from managers who are asking what services will be available for employees who are expressing concern, getting nervous. What can we offer them?
14				<<Caller name, title, dept>>	I have numerous important reports in the J Drive and they seem to be inaccessible. I am worried that the files will be corrupted. Who can help me? If I can't get to them, this will cost us a fortune!
15				<<Caller name, title, dept>>	I was logged on my VOIP phone and all of a sudden was booted off. Since then I can't log into my phone, and it's getting close to some of our critical deadlines. What am I supposed to do?

SAMPLE BUSINESS UNIT INJECTS

CALL #	TIME	DESIGN TEAM MEMBER (SIMULATOR)	ROUTING	CALLER'S NAME, TITLE & DEPT	CALL SCRIPT
16				<<Caller name, title, dept>>	IT has requested that several of my employees shut down their workstations. We are down to 8 laptops to complete the work. So far we are okay, but I'm just giving you a heads-up. How long it will be before we can use them again? If something doesn't change in the next hour, I might as well send them all home.
17				<<Caller name, title, dept>>	My <<app>> session gave me an abnormal session timeout and now I can't log back in. What's going on?
18				<<Caller name, title, dept>>	I'm calling again because I want to get ready for the worst case, but since I'm new, I have no idea what our alternatives are. What if we lose all system access? Do we have manual procedures? If so, I have no idea what they are. Can anybody give is some assistance?
19				<<Caller name, title, dept>>	I have tried logging into SAP, but the system is stunningly slow. Have we been hacked?
20				<<Caller name, title, dept>>	We normally get alarm pages through the exchanger server within a minute. I just received an alarm after 35 minutes. What's happening? Why aren't we getting any communications?
21				<<Caller name, title, dept>>	I am working on a critical document for the President and have tried to save it, but the system will not let me save the file. I spent a lot of time on the document; I don't want to lose it. How do I save it?

CYBER BREACH 77

SAMPLE BUSINESS UNIT INJECTS

CALL #	TIME	DESIGN TEAM MEMBER (SIMULATOR)	ROUTING	CALLER'S NAME, TITLE & DEPT	CALL SCRIPT
22				<<Caller name, title, dept>>	My desktop screen went blank and then normal – I can't see the mouse cursor anywhere. What do I do? No one is answering the Help Desk line – I need help!
23				<<Caller name, title, dept>>	I removed my laptop from the cradle to work in the conference room, and I can't connect to the network. The wi-fi is on but the drives are missing in the directory. What's going on?
24				<<Caller name, title, dept>>	I'm trying to accept a calendar appointment for next week, but when I press the 'accept' button, nothing happens. And when I try and reboot the screen freezes. Something really strange is going on. I am not getting any information from IT.

Technology timeline

It is exceedingly helpful to have the Technology team establish a timeline to craft their story and subsequent failures. A simple sample timeline might look like this:

TECHNOLOGY TIMELINE		
DATE / TIME	SYSTEM	EVENT
T-120		Healthy state
T-119		Initial compromise
T-118		▶ Rooting of systems – the progression of what goes on over the "rooting" time could include things like this: ▶ The virus has now compromised approximately <<%>> of the systems, giving visibility, as well as command and control access, to infected systems from outside the company via encrypted SSL. ▶ The Bad Guy can see what is being typed, gaining passwords and privilege to system's along the way. ▶ The Bad Guy is infecting workstations as well as servers using the same payload. ▶ The Bad Guy is going through the systems, deciding what data they want to take.
T-0		Attack begins in earnest
T+ 0:10	Network	The company's internet connections are SUPER slow. It is taking forever to do anything.
T+0:15	Website	Five company web pages are defaced.

Key injects

There are likely several injects that are critical to the story – ones you will want to keep track of and know how they were resolved. EMSS refers to those as "key injects." They are designed to raise specific issues you want to follow during the exercise to learn how the players resolve them. A cyber exercise could easily have four or five key injects that need to be followed from inject delivery to resolution (or the end of the exercise). They should somehow be indicated on your inject sheet so you or your observers are able to follow them. Bold or italicized type, colored font, or a shaded row could suffice to make the key injects stand out from the others.

*Storytelling is an essential human activity.
The harder the situation, the more essential it is.*
— *Tim O'Brien*

Final review

Once the injects have been fully vetted by all the team members, there is still a bit of work to do: The injects now need to be prepared for their delivery on exercise day. This entails the following:
- ▶ Put the injects into the sequence that they will be delivered. It's likely that your in-process inject sheet is grouped by the persons or organizations who wrote the injects. You will need to review the topics and determine which get delivered earlier or later. Some will be dependent on other injects or the overall exercise story.
- ▶ Determine and assign the time you want the injects to be delivered (i.e. delivery cadence). Depending on how many injects you have, the experience of the team, and the complexity of the injects, this could be range from one inject a minute (or less) to one inject every two minutes or longer.
- ▶ Assign a Simulation Team member to deliver the call. Select a name from the Sim Team list to place each call. When ever possible, it is always a good idea to match Simulation Team member based on their skills to a specific inject to ensure it is played out as well as it can be.

Before anything else, preparation is the key to success.
— *Alexander Graham Bell*

Sample message form

For advanced tabletop exercises, EMSS will often transfer injects from the master list to individual message forms. These forms are given to specific individuals or teams for them to resolve.

To resolve them, they review the inject, discuss possible solutions with their team mates and then go over to the Simulator who is in the back of the room. The Simulator "magically" turns into the person who is making the call that is on the message form and role-plays the call. The exercise player then has to work with the Simulator to resolve the issue.

This may sound odd, but playing out this interaction is very helpful, and it provides powerful learnings to the exercise players. In a basic tabletop exercise, you simply talk about what you "would do" to solve the problem. In an advanced tabletop, you actually have to talk to someone to solve the problem; thus, there is an opportunity for questions, rebuttals and push-back. This is a significant learning experience as it makes them think more deeply about the problem and how to solve it. That is an understanding that and can only come in a simulated exercise.

EXERCISE MESSAGE FORM

Date/Time: <<date>>, <<time>>   **Tracking #** <<inject #>>

Name of caller:

Routing:

To resolve this problem, please see: <<name of Sim Team member>>

Message

Action taken/ Next steps:

Summary

Well-crafted and vetted exercise injects are tied to the exercise objectives and deliverables, and continue to develop the exercise story. Injects delivered using different methods – phone calls, emails, text messages, etc. – can make for a more engaging and interesting experience. Thoughtful and well-designed exercise injects will help you reach your exercise objectives.

CHAPTER NINE

Make your exercise "public" for greater impact

Chapter goals:
1. Learn how to use traditional and social media to tell the story.
2. Understand how to use audio/visual injects to progress your exercise story.
3. Identify how radio broadcasts and news video can improve your narrative.
4. Explore the use of video for maximum impact in telling your narrative.

One key concern of Senior Executives is how the company can manage the brand and reputation fallout that is likely to occur when a breach is made public. In your exercise, you want to make sure that the team has to deal with those issues, so it is necessary to expose or "out" the event.

I strongly suggest involving the "media" in the exercise – not literally of course, but figuratively. In our exercise world-of-make believe, making the "media" aware of the cyber incident adds another challenging and very valuable dimension to the training. Factoring in the media requires the exercise players to develop messaging and communications to manage your organizations reputation and the brand impact of the cyber incident.

In the 'real world,' for many cyber incidents, no one knows that a breach has occurred, sometimes not even the breached company itself. Until either the company comes forward to acknowledge it, or the hacker exposes the company to the rest of the world, nothing has happened — at least as far as the public is aware.

Showing that a company has cyber security and data protection measures in place is critical to maintaining customer loyalty and to protecting your company's brand reputation. A recent *Forbes Insights* report[28] demon-

---
28 Forbes Insights – "Fallout: The Reputational Impact of IT Risk"http://www-935.ibm.com/services/multimedia/RLL12363USEN_2014_Forbes_Insights.pdf

strated how a cyber incident can have serious repercussions in how the public perceives the company. A few chilling statistics in the report:
- ▶ 46% of organizations suffered damage to their reputations and brand value as a result of a cyber-security breach.
- ▶ 19% of organizations suffered damage to their reputations and brand value as a result of a third-party security breach or IT system failure.

Turning the spotlight on potential media coverage will be painful, but it is a critical aspect of the exercise.

> *Expect the best, plan for the worst,*
> *and prepare to be surprised.*
> *— Denis Waitley*

Social media

Social media injects need to be a big part of your exercise. Words and images spread rapidly on Twitter, Facebook, YouTube, Instagram, and many other social media platforms. Social media is how much of our communication circumnavigates the globe. It is still an area where many companies are hesitant to communicate, especially during a crisis. It is however, a critical activity for your Communications Team to have to deal with in the exercise.
- ▶ Has your Communications Team thought through a cyber incident?
- ▶ Who will speak for the organization and under what circumstances?
- ▶ What type of messaging templates does your Communications Team have?
- ▶ Who approves the releases?
- ▶ Do they have templates for 140-character messages suitable for posting on Twitter?

Hopefully, before your exercise the team can prepare templates to practice with. If they don't, during the exercise they will find themselves trying to develop messages on the fly, and if you have enough social media injects they will feel like they are drinking out of a fire hose.

EMSS places social media injects on a single sheet of paper with the logo of the platform on the page. The Communications Team is instructed to respond to them as they would any real social media message. We ask them to record their responses on the inject form and return them to the facilitator at the end of the exercise.

SOCIAL MEDIA SAMPLES

twitter

Posted by @MediaMaven

ABC Corp hacked – major release of sensitive customer info. #ABCCorpHack Were U impacted?

---

facebook

I have been treated terribly by ABC Corp which lost my data and now doesn't I return my calls. Typical company, they just want your money but when they do something wrong they are nowhere in sight. I think we should start a cyber boycott! Has this happened to anybody else? #ABCCorpHack

---

The perils of social media

Social media can be a tricky playing field and your team needs practice. Erring on the side of humanity and reliability will minimize the damage and possibly gain the company some respect, even if your execution isn't initially the smoothest. What people want is businesses to be truthful and real and timely. Focus on clear communications that are transparent and honest. Work with your legal team on crafting communications and use this exercise as an opportunity for your team to practice.

> *Let our advance worrying become*
> *advance thinking and planning*
> *— Winston Churchill*

Using media tools to progress the story

EMSS normally plots narratives out using the phases as discussed in Chapter 7, and then uses audio-visual tools to progress the story. Here is an example of how that might look:

SOURCE	MODE OF DELIVERY	AV #	EXERCISE TIME H : M	CONTENT
Perpetrator	Email or video	1	00:30	Mildly threatening, no demonstration that the perpetrator is in the systems.
Perpetrator	Email or video	2	01:30	Ratchets up the rhetoric. Perp tweets "I'm gonna show you!" on Twitter; (Twitter logo appears on the video.)
News media	Video or radio	3	02:00	Perpetrator's email of video #2 is released to news outlets. <<News channel>> is en route to company to talk to executives.
Perpetrator	Email or video	4	03:00	Very threatening tone, and now shows proof of being in the systems. Demonstrates she/he has customer data and Social Security Numbers.
News media	Video or radio	5	03:30	<<News channel>> broadcasts report that the perp has gotten into the systems and thousands of customers have had information compromised and released to dark web sites.

As you can see, the "perp" starts out with a mildly threatening tone. He doesn't demonstrate that he is in the systems, he just says he is. This could be some young kid in a garage playing with you; at this point, you don't know. Keep it only mildly threatening at first to keep the team from going into full-blown panic right away. After all, in an exercise everyone "knows" the situation is going to get worse, so they have a tendency to throw everything at it right off the bat.

At this point, it's important to say that you, as the facilitator, need to keep the exercise players honest. If management is ready to go all out now, you can let them do so, but, seriously – would they really? The facilitator can help the team from jumping the gun by asking them theoretical questions (like, "do you really want to do that?") and injecting a bit of reality if they start to overreact.

In the table above you can see how the story is progressed through the audio-visual injects, while at the same time, other injects would continue to be delivered via phone or paper (depending on your exercise). In this table, the media became aware of the incident because AV inject #2 was released to Twitter by the perpetrator. (This is a great way to place the breach in the public eye, first to social media, then to traditional media, and the story can progress from there.)

Radio and television broadcasts

The best audio-visual tools for enhancing the cyber exercise experience and progressing the story are:

- ▶ Radio broadcasts: A low-cost, effective option.
- ▶ Television broadcasts: EMSS' favorite method. Really hits on all cylinders: more "real", powerful, feels more visceral, gripping, and information rich.

Radio broadcast

The radio broadcast is a powerful tool and can be used to set the stage at the beginning of the exercise. It can clearly demonstrate to the exercise players that the media, and therefore the public, is now aware of the cyber incident.

Starting the exercise with a broadcast can really set the tone and put the players into the mindset that this situation has really happened and that the public is aware. The initial broadcast usually reiterates some of the basic information that's contained in the exercise plan narrative and should include a few twists such as "our reporter is in route to ABC Company to speak with company executives." This can be helpful as the players are just starting to "wrap their brain" around the incident; they need to get engaged rapidly.

If you have some major twists in the middle of the exercise, consider using a broadcast to introduce those as "breaking news" stories. These should be short broadcasts – as little as 90 seconds and not more than two minutes. The goal is to drop this new information into the mix by a "reporter" who quickly updates the situation and then says "back to the studio." This can heighten the energy level of the players, get participants' blood pumping again, and reinvigorate the situation.

Begin by determining which radio station will be "broadcasting" the story. Would this incident have national implications? In that case, it may be from a national network. Is it a more local event? Then it would more likely be covered by your local radio or TV news stations. Pick an appropriate station and listen to them to get a sense of their style, what they are like, and how their broadcasters sound.

Plan your broadcast to be between 90 seconds and two minutes but no longer than three minutes. People's attention will drift away if you go too much longer than that. If you plan to do the broadcast yourself, write the script, then practice it saying it aloud several times before recording. This practice will serve you well when it comes time to record. A story that reads well on paper may sound awkward and stilted when spoken.

EMSS is lucky enough to have access to a fabulous Bay Area voice-over talent with his own studio to produce our broadcasts. He records them, adds appropriate sound effects, mixes them, and then sends them to our office via email as an MP3 file. You may be able to find a similar resource at a local college from their broadcasting program or similar sources.

Television

Video production is highly effective but more expensive. If a picture is worth a thousand words, then moving pictures must be worth a few million. An opening television video can be an even more powerful way to kick off your exercise. EMSS makes them in the style of many of the hacker videos – the perpetrator is disguised, the voice is altered, and the image might even have blurry images.

Create the script for the television bulletin in the same way as you would a radio broadcast. If you are acquiring video images from a variety of sources, check that the image quality is the same. Mixing professional video stock footage with video pulled from YouTube can work, but you may need to spend a lot of time to make it flow seamlessly. There are many stock video companies on the Internet to provide footage, and many video production companies who can do the work for you. Be aware, however, that it could get costly.

The Chinese use two brush strokes to write the word 'crisis. One brush stroke stands for danger; the other for opportunity. In a crisis, be aware of the danger - but recognize the opportunity.
— ***John F Kennedy***

Summary

The goal of an audio-visual inject is to impart a feeling of realism. In the case of a cyber exercise, it can demonstrate that the media, and therefore the general public, is aware of your cyber incident. A well-crafted audio-visual inject will not only move the story line along but help instill a sense of reality and urgency to your exercise as well. It is worth budgeting for some professional assistance to really make this exercise come alive.

CHAPTER TEN

The team that makes it happen, the Exercise Team

Chapter goals:
1. See how an exercise team can make an exercise come alive.
2. Understand the role of the Exercise Facilitator.
3. Review the Simulation Team structure and determine what you will need in your exercise.
4. Consider the Observer and Exercise Assistant roles and assess if you will need them in your exercise
5. Learn about "teachable moments."

Who are they?

Now that the exercise design is done, you need to be thinking about how you are doing to deliver it. Actually, I would hope that you've been thinking about that in tandem with the design efforts. Hopefully, you have already signed up your Exercise Design Team members as Simulators or Observers. If not, stop right now and go ask them – or find others if you need more people.

The Exercise Team, the cast of characters you need to make your exercise work on the "big day," is critical. You may not need the entire list below, but for a big exercise you might. For an Advanced Tabletop exercise, your Exercise Team will likely be a smaller group; however, with a Functional or Full-scale exercise, it's possible there will be a lot of people. The Exercise Team is usually comprised of the following positions:
- Exercise Facilitator
- Simulation Team
- Observers
- Exercise Assistant(s)

The following chart clarifies the roles needed for each type of exercise:

POSITION	ADVANCED TABLETOP	FUNCTIONAL	FULL-SCALE
Exercise Facilitator	Yes	Yes	Yes
Simulation Team Coordinator	No	Maybe	Yes
Simulation Team	Yes	Yes	Yes
Simulation Team Scribe	No	Maybe	Yes
Observer	Yes	Yes	Yes
Exercise Assistant(s)	No	Maybe	Yes

The way a team plays as a whole determines its success. You may have the greatest bunch of individual stars in the world, but if they don't play together, the club won't be worth a dime.
— *Babe Ruth*

Exercise Facilitator

Who is the Exercise Facilitator? A variety of different folks can play this critical position. This role could be you, the reader...a BCP, IT or Info Sec Manager...or an outside source. Sometimes, someone from the outside can point things out and/or say things that need to be said that an insider would be reluctant to mention.

Think of the Exercise Facilitator as a combination of an orchestra conductor and traffic cop. The common responsibilities of the Exercise Facilitator include:

- Design process.
- Leads the entire design process – pretty much everything in this book.
- Exercise day:
  > Kicks off the exercise – Opens the exercise by reviewing the structure of the day, the exercise plan and scenario, and associated documents.
  > Facilitates the exercise – Acts as the main (or only) Facilitator

on exercise day[28]. Is responsible for the event from start to finish, including oversight of all players, and intervening (as necessary) during the "play time," observing and monitoring issues that need attention (such as injects gone awry or key injects being ignored).
  > Manages the inject flow – Like Goldilocks, the cadence of inject delivery should be not too hot and not too cold, but just the right pace to ensure a suitable amount of tension and angst in the room.
  > Conducts the debrief – Leads the exercise players in the debrief session at the end.
- After-action Report (AAR):
  > Writes the After-action Report – either as the primary or sole author.
  > Reviews exercise findings with appropriate parties – Prepares and delivers AAR and other reports to entities within the organization on the exercise findings. Reviews the project plan for remediation.
- Tracking and follow-up (this may or may not be the role of the Facilitator, depending on your company):
  > Track progress of remediation efforts identified following the exercise – May be tasked with following up (or creating) on a project plan for remediation efforts and reporting progress of those efforts.

Simulation Team

You need a Simulation Team for all Advanced Tabletop, Functional and Full-scale exercises. The Simulation Team ("Sim Team") is the driver of the exercise, and can often make or break it. It will be delivering all the injects and will become the "face of the exercise" to the players. No matter how great your exercise design, it's your Simulation Team that will make it shine (or not).

---

28 There are instances where two or more facilitators is required. Examples include multiple sites, important groups such as senior leadership teams or particularly challenging teams that you want to make sure stay on point and engaged

Simulation Team organization
The Simulation Team may have three positions:
- ▶ Simulation Team Coordinator
- ▶ Simulation Team member
- ▶ Simulation Team Scribe

Simulation Team Coordinator

In a large exercise, it is critical to have a Simulation Team Coordinator to oversee the Simulation room and the activities in it. Coordinator responsibilities are to:
- ▶ Serve as the eyes and ears of the Exercise Facilitator.
- ▶ Connect the Simulation Team to the Facilitator and Observers.
- ▶ Assist the Simulation Team in developing responses and making up spontaneous injects.
- ▶ Monitor the flow of the injects and keep the Simulation Team on track with the inject delivery cadence.
- ▶ Serve as the Simulation Team contact point-person if something needs to be followed up on, an inject needs to be "righted," or an inject needs to be re-delivered.
- ▶ Provide general coaching help to Simulators.

Simulation Team member

A Simulation Team member has the following responsibilities:
- ▶ Understand the main responsibilities of the Sim Team – how to play the "outside world", deliver their assigned injects, and insert them on time.
- ▶ Know the exercise narrative, injects, timeline and story progression. In other words, know the exercise scenario narrative, from start to end
- ▶ Follow instructions from the Sim Team Coordinator (if present).
- ▶ Provide realistic time frames to players. For example, if the Simulator is playing a reporter, a realistic time frame for a deadline might be one hour but not ten minutes.
- ▶ Develop realistic spontaneous injects.

Simulation Team Scribe

The Simulation Team Scribe has the following responsibilities:
- ▶ Know the exercise narrative, injects, timeline and story progression. In other words, know the exercise scenario narrative, from start to end
- ▶ Record facts as requested by the Sim Coordinator or Sim Team members. This helps to keep everyone on track and telling them same story.

What makes a good Simulation Team participant?

While many people can be a Sim Team member, an outstanding Simulator will have the following qualities:
- ▶ Have a good overall knowledge of the company and the business. (The more they understand the organization and how it really works, the better Simulator they will be.)
- ▶ Have a good knowledge of the processes and procedures used within the specific departments that are being exercised. (This is critical when exercising groups such as Facilities, IT, or critical lines of business. You just can't make those things up.)
- ▶ Possess a good attitude, be creative, and be a team player. (Even the shyest folks can really get into their Sim role after just a few minutes.)
- ▶ Produce "credible stories" when speaking with players and stay on course with the exercise plan.

I am often asked how many Sim Team members are needed. For a cyber exercise, it is not so much a certain number that is needed, but rather the necessary knowledge. Because of the technology aspects of a cyber exercise, you need to make sure you have the right technology folks in the Sim Team. My short list would include people representing:
- ▶ Information Security
- ▶ Infrastructure
- ▶ Applications Development and Support
- ▶ Network
- ▶ Database
- ▶ Key lines of business

- Corporate Communications
- Human Resources
- Facilities
- Physical security

Simulation Team location

In an Advanced Tabletop, the Simulation Team should be located in the room, likely behind a long table. For a Functional or Full-scale exercise, place them in a separate room. It is always better to have them all together in one room rather than making calls from their office or disparate locations. This allows them to hear what the others are saying and follow the progression of the exercise. It also gives you a lot more control to have a team located in a centralized location. Having said that, space and telephony constraints may dictate the need to have a dispersed team. If that is the case, communication between and among team members will be critical. This could be done via instant messaging, open conference bridge and/or a chat board.

Delivering and receiving injects via phone calls

There are two rules for Sim Team members to follow when working the phones in an exercise:

- When starting the delivery of any call, they should *ALWAYS* start the phone message with the phrase, "This is an exercise message." It is possible that the Sim Team member might mis-dial the number and tell some unsuspecting person about the horrible thing that has just happened. Starting with "This is an exercise message" gets everyone on the same page right off the bat, and can avoid creating another War of the Worlds[29] scenario.
- When picking up the phone, they should *ALWAYS* answer the phone with "May I help you?" The Sim Team member has no idea who the person on the other end is looking for. They could be calling back

---

29 "The War of the Worlds" was an episode of the Mercury Theater on the Air. It was performed on October 30, 1938, aired over the CBS radio network, and was directed and narrated by Orson Wells. The episode was an adaptation of H. G. Wells' novel *The War of the Worlds*. The legend is that millions were lead into thinking there was a Martian invasion underway. They myth is greater than reality. "The Myth of the War of the Worlds Panic", Slate Magazine, October 28, 2013 http://www.slate.com/articles/arts/history/2013/10/orson_welles_war_of_the_worlds_panic_myth_the_infamous_radio_broadcast_did.html

regarding an inject or they could be expecting the answerer to play someone in the "outside world." If they start rambling, or the Sim Team member is not sure who or what they are looking for, they should be stopped right away and asked, "Who are you looking for?" The caller should be able to respond with something like, "I am looking for Al's Car Service." The Sim Team member can then reply, "Hi, this is Al; how can I help you?" This quickly gets everyone on track and the call is off on a good foot.

No Martians!

Going back to the War of the Worlds scenario, EMSS has one non-negotiable rule in the art of simulation: *NO MARTIAN LANDINGS!* This is meant as a reminder to the Simulation Team to stay in line with the exercise flow, narrative, and injects. I have found that occasionally the Sim Team becomes overly enthusiastic about this world they are creating, and the next thing you know, they are adding in unexpected situations and issues that weren't agreed on in the design meetings, such as an unnecessary power outage, an additional dead employee, or a second explosion. Anything that varies from the overall direction of the exercise needs to be cleared by the Exercise Facilitator (or Sim Team Coordinator). So, please – no Martians!

Observers

As the title implies, the Observer role performs the primary evaluation job of the exercise. The Observer role has the following responsibilities:
- ▶ Understands the role of the team that he or she is assigned to evaluate.
- ▶ Knows and understands the exercise plan and injects.
- ▶ Monitors key injects (Chapter 8) and provides feedback until they are successfully resolved.
- ▶ Has a clear sense of the exercise timeline and story progression, where the exercise is going.
- ▶ Provides feedback to the Simulation Team on inject issues.
- ▶ Offers focused and objective observations.
- ▶ Reports to the Exercise Facilitator.

> *It doesn't work to leap a twenty-foot chasm
> in two ten-foot jumps.*
> — **Unknown source**

Tracking key injects

Observers also have the job of tracking the key injects. Here are a few suggestions on how to track them:

- ▶ Each key inject should be assigned to a specific observer, who will follow its progress until resolution.
- ▶ The Observer should note on their observation form how the inject was handled.
- ▶ When a key inject is due to be delivered, stand near the individual or team assigned to receive it to note how it is being handled as it comes in.
- ▶ In an Advanced Tabletop, Observers can hand out the injects to their team on the prescribed schedule.
- ▶ Take note of how it is being handled. Is someone working on it, actively trying to get it resolved? Or is it just sitting there, unnoticed and unaddressed?
  - > If it's being worked on, take notes as to how it's being resolved.
  - > If it's being ignored, alert the Sim Team. They can call in the inject again – and again, and again – until it has been addressed properly.
- ▶ Check in with the Sim Team for their feedback.

Exercise Assistants

Exercise Assistants are most often used in Full-scale exercises and provide another valuable set of hands to perform tasks during the exercise. (If you have the budget, an assistant is useful in a smaller exercise as well.) Some of the activities assigned to an assistant may include:

- ▶ Playing any audio-visual injects as in noted in the exercise script.
- ▶ Handing out any paper materials, including the exercise plan, any news stories "pulled from the web," or the participant evaluations.
- ▶ Making phone calls on behalf of the exercise Facilitator to check in

with other locations, the Simulation Team, or others as necessary.
- ▶ Checking in with the Facilitator frequently.
- ▶ Keeping the exercise clock set to "exercise time" (if you have changed the time in the exercise plan).
- ▶ Assisting with the debriefing session by recording the debrief notes.
- ▶ Collecting the evaluation and observation forms.

Exercise Team orientation session

A solid orientation session will take roughly 90 minutes to two hours. The good news is that you can probably have one meeting with the entire Exercise Team together – Simulators, Observers, and Assistants – to cover many of the same points across the roles. Here is a typical agenda to cover information applicable to all:
- ▶ Go over the roles and responsibilities particular to each role.
- ▶ Talk through the exercise plan, overall injects, and key injects.
- ▶ Review any specific forms you are to use in the course of the exercise.
- ▶ Plot strategy and methods for escalation of issues.
- ▶ Complete written evaluation at the end of the exercise.
- ▶ Ask everyone to arrive at least 30 minutes before the start of the exercise on exercise day. This allows them plenty of time to get settled in and set up before the exercise begins.

Key points to emphasize to Sim Team members

Inject delivery
- ▶ Deliver each inject at its scheduled time. Although most injects are not so time-sensitive that being a few minutes off will result in the crashing failure of your exercise, the exercise can get bogged down if someone is chronically late delivering their injects.
- ▶ Develop a list of additional caller names in advance to avoid dropping in famous or infamous people's names in a rush to respond to the caller.
- ▶ Stay in line with the exercise script and objectives – no Martians.
- ▶ Note any key injects that have been assigned. (Part of the Simula-

tion Team's job is to keep them alive until resolved properly.)

Organization
- ▶ Stay organized. Simulation Team members should find a way to keep control over the exercise plan(s) and injects, such as using a binder or clipboard.
- ▶ Highlight their assigned injects and make sure they are clear about them, including the intent of each inject, how to deliver them, and their ability to answer any corresponding questions.
- ▶ Keep notes on what they said and the caller's response. Remembering all the made-up stories is difficult; they shouldn't rely on their memory afterwards. Truth is easy to remember; lies, not so much!

Acting skills
Sim Team members should:
- ▶ React convincingly to the inject recipients' comments.
- ▶ Respond to a participant's requests/actions and repeat information if asked.
- ▶ Confer with others. If a Sim Team member needs help developing a response, they should put the caller on hold, consult with teammates (and the Coordinator, if present), and then respond. They will be surrounded by lots of people who can help craft a good story.

Work with the rest of the team
- ▶ Be sure to keep the Sim Team Coordinator informed of any spontaneous stories that are created, or any emerging issues that may have come up in the calls.
- ▶ Keep the Sim Team Scribe informed of impromptu stories so they can be recorded and tracked.

Maintain their health
- ▶ Pace themselves. Working as a Sim Team member can be very tiring. It's a lot of fun, yes, but draining.
- ▶ Stay hydrated, drink lots of fluids. This will also help avoid anyone from losing their voice.

Key points to emphasize to observers

The evaluation process
- ▶ Review individual Observer assignments. Each Observer should be familiar with the team they are assigned to oversee.
- ▶ Check any key injects the team is assigned to receive. Develop an approach to take if the team fails to respond appropriately.
- ▶ Monitor exercise play and relate it to the exercise objectives and expected outcomes. Evaluate ***actions,*** not ***people.***
- ▶ Determine if objectives and related actions are met.

Evaluation methods
- ▶ Observe and evaluate what the participants do.
- ▶ Look at situation boards and reporting forms.
- ▶ Look at any reports.
- ▶ Talk with participants as necessary to ensure clarity, but avoid giving direction; your role is to observe, not to become an unofficial player.
- ▶ Attend all briefings the team you are observing may hold.
- ▶ Be a "fly on the wall" to listen into conversations and informal briefings.

> *The purpose of life is to listen - to yourself,*
> *to your neighbor, to your world and to God*
> *and, when the time comes, to respond in as helpful*
> *a way as you can find...from within and without.*
> — ***Mr. (Fred) Rogers,***
> *1928-2003, American educator, minister and television host*

"Teachable moments"

In any exercise, there will be "teachable moments." These are moments when you see the team struggling, and you possess information that could move them farther along if only you would share it. Any member of the Exercise Team may be able to assist the exercise players with a teachable moment. Of course, you could withhold that information and just let them hit the wall – that's one type of exercise learning.

However, another way to approach this situation is to provide just enough information to get them unstuck, then stand back and watch them go on their way again. Why would you choose this approach? Shouldn't you wait for them to find their own way? After all, aren't they supposed to learn from this experience?

Yes, you want them to learn, but look at it this way: You don't have exercises very often. If you could provide them some basic information or a moment of reflection that allows them to get "unstuck," they actually have a better chance of going farther in the exercise and learning more.

I tell my Exercise Team that if they see the players struggling and not able to move forward, they have permission to try to "unstick" them by providing some data or asking a pointed question that may help them rethink the situation and move forward.

Note the difference between this kind of indirect help, and simply giving someone an answer. With the former, they are given a clue with which they can get back on track; with the latter, they are given the solution.

Summary

The Exercise Team is the group in charge of taking your carefully crafted exercise and delivering it to the players. Their role is critical to the success of your exercise. Carefully select, train, and coach these individuals to ensure that they will help you achieve the goals and objectives of the exercise.

CHAPTER 11

Leading up to the Big Day

Chapter goals:
1. Review the basics of room selection and layout.
2. Learn a simple way to keep all exercise documentation organized.
3. Prepare a catering list to include healthy foods, snacks and beverages.
4. Develop a document summary page to make document reproduction a breeze.
5. Design the appropriate pre-exercise training to make sure everyone is prepared for the big day.
6. Know what to send out as a reminder for all exercise players.
7. Remember to take time for your own personal preparedness.

Good on you! You have mastered the design process and the exercise is set to go! Great job! This is, however, no time to sit back on your laurels – you've still got lots of work to do. This chapter is about all of the things you need to do to get you to the starting line in great shape! Luckily, it's a short list:
- ▶ Room selection and set-up
- ▶ Catering and A/V
- ▶ Document preparation
- ▶ Pre-exercise training
- ▶ Exercise player reminders
- ▶ Your personal preparation.

Before anything else, preparation is the key to success.
— *Alexander Graham Bell*

The Room
Exercise room selection
This topic is included towards the end of the book, but to be clear, you should have booked the exercise rooms long ago, back at the beginning during the exercise planning stage. (See the Appendix for exercise timelines.)

Most companies do not have a dedicated Emergency Operations Center (EOC). They may use a traditional conference room ("cold site"), or a pre-designated conference room or area that has supplies preorganized and allocated for their expressed use ("warm site"). If you have any of these facilities in place, ideally, you would use it for the exercise. This would help test and improve the site for real activations.

More than likely, you will be using a conference or training room. Make sure that it is large enough for the exercise players, the Simulation Team, and catering.

> *If it's at all possible, try to set up the room the day before. If anything is amiss, you'll be grateful for the extra time to fix it.*

Exercise room set-up
It is always preferable to do the room set-up the day before the exercise. This prevents those last-minute issues that can lead to increases in your blood pressure and anxiety level. Who needs that? It also allows you to get a better night's rest before the exercise. Here is a short list of items to consider when doing the room set-up:

- **Equipment and supplies:**
    - Validate the equipment list, and ensure everything that was ordered is now available.
    - Identify the location of the closest copier and fax machine. Check that they work properly.
    - Make sure there are sufficient flip charts, markers, and masking tape available for use as status boards (also check with Facilities to see if your room has any restrictions on taping things to the walls; that has been a senstive subject with some of our clients).
    - Set up a sign-in table. (Pre-printed sign-in sheets are not only

helpful, they provide a good audit trail).
- > Prepare any necessary identifying directional signs. If you organize the players by teams, make table tents with the team names (i.e., Operations, Logistics, Finance, Planning & Intelligence, and Command).
- > Set out table tent signage for team(s) and/or individual seating.

▶ **Phones:**
- > Install and test all lines and handsets. (Yes, every line and every device.)
- > Ensure phone numbers in the phone directory are mapped to the correct handset.
- > If conducting any audio-conference briefings (for example, an executive or multi-site briefing), ensure that an appropriate speakerphone (or equivalent) is available and works properly.

▶ **A/V:**
- > Verify all equipment/devices that will be used to play any audio broadcasts or visual presentations (e.g., slides or video) are working properly.
- > If you will have a large audience, arrange for a microphone and speaker. A wireless hand-held or lavalier-type is best.
- > Make sure the visual presentation materials can be seen and heard from every position in the room. Insufficient space can seriously impair the effectiveness of this strategically important and intense experience and risk the return on the investment.
- > If that's not possible due to the room size or layout, try to find a place that can accommodate the most number of players.
- > Have a still-picture camera available. Make sure the batteries are fresh and there is room on the memory card for a substantial number of pictures.

If you will be holding a mock press conference, have a video camera set up in an appropriate place (or ready to be set up at the right time). Again, make sure the batteries are fresh and there is room on the memory card or tape to last through the scheduled time.

Advanced tabletop room layout

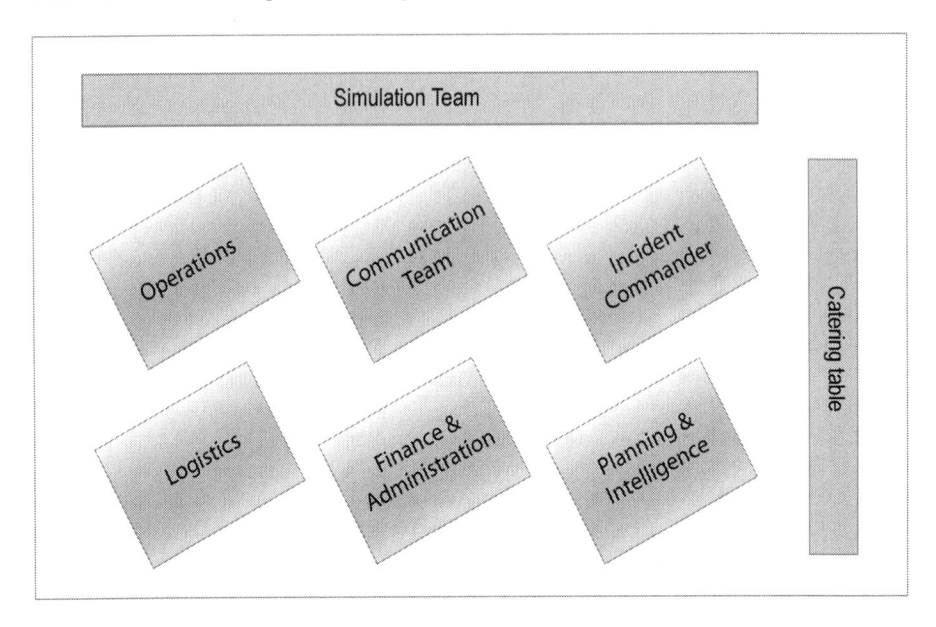

```
┌─────────────────────────────────────────────────┐
│         [ Simulation Team ]                     │
│                                                 │
│   Operations   Communication   Incident         │
│                   Team         Commander        │
│                                         Catering│
│                                          table  │
│   Logistics    Finance &      Planning &        │
│                Administration Intelligence      │
└─────────────────────────────────────────────────┘
```

Functional or full-scale room layout

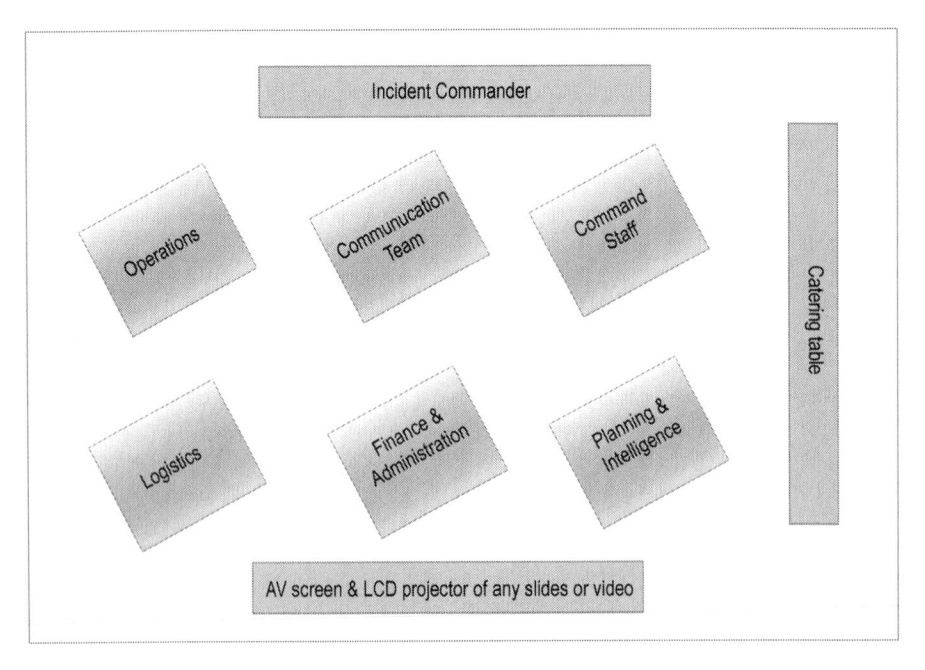

```
┌─────────────────────────────────────────────────┐
│         [ Incident Commander ]                  │
│                                                 │
│   Operations   Communucation   Command          │
│                   Team         Staff            │
│                                         Catering│
│                                          table  │
│   Logistics    Finance &      Planning &        │
│                Administration Intelligence      │
│                                                 │
│   [ AV screen & LCD projector of any slides or video ] │
└─────────────────────────────────────────────────┘
```

Simulation room set-up (Functional or Full-Scale exercise)

Ideally, the Sim Team room will be near the exercise room but completely separated and far enough away so the team players can't hear the Simulators – so a shared wall would not be the best thing. It is important to have the following:

- ▶ Adequately-sized room and wall space.
  - > For 5 – 10 Simulators: A U-shaped table is a great room layout. This allows the Coordinator to "walk the room" in the middle so she or he can eavesdrop on the calls and keep track of the action.
  - > For 11+ Simulators: Classroom style seating or tables against the wall with Simulator backs to the center of the room works well. This allows the Sim Team Coordinator to move easily around the space and helps dampen the sound.
- ▶ Sufficient landline phones.
  - > Each Sim Team member must have their own phone. Ideally, there should be a hold button, but no voicemail, and the phones should not roll to another line if it is busy when dialled.
  - > Cell phones are not ideal. Remember that batteries can die, reception can be dodgy, and lost calls happen on even the most "on" network. Providing each Simulator with a landline handset avoids those problems. In addition, whether using a company cell phone or a personal one, the Sim Team member may receive non-exercise calls, which would be very disruptive.
- ▶ White boards or flip charts are needed for scribes to note the current status, important spontaneous injects, or new data from the players.

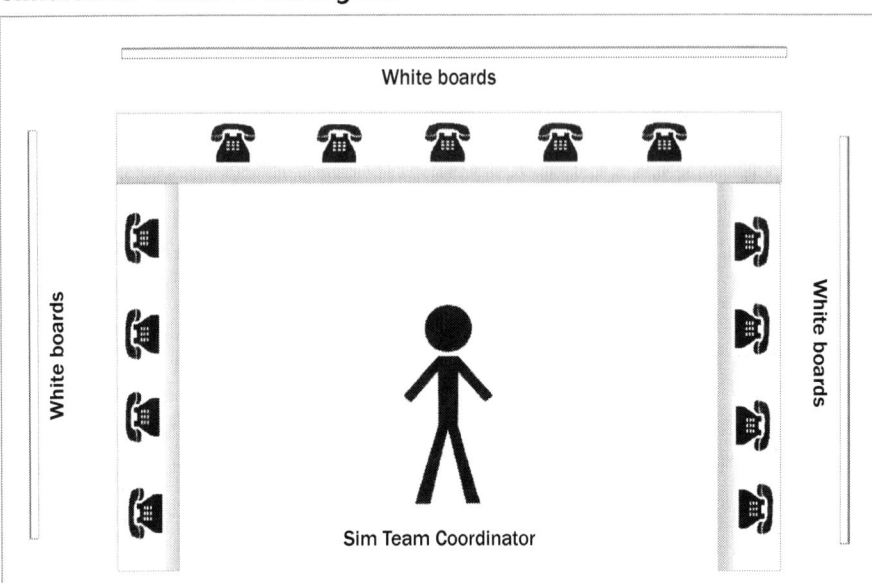

Simulation Team room layout

Sim Team room for a functional or full-scale exercise

Catering and Audio/Visual

Audio/Visual

Ask to have an A/V technician available at least 30 minutes before the exercise start time and on-call throughout the day. This gives you a bit of insurance in case issues pop up at the last minute. Before you start, check to be sure that all A/V materials play correctly.

Catering

Food is an important part of any exercise. You can have a great exercise but if the food is lousy, the participants will be talking about it for months to come. I recommend healthy food options whenever possible, and avoid greasy, smelly, and/or messy foods. Heavy foods are hard to digest and slow people down.

- ▶ Morning: Refreshments including coffee, tea, water and something to eat such as muffins, fruit, bagels, or energy bars.
- ▶ Lunch: Box lunches are fast and easy for people to grab and keep

working if necessary, or to eat during the debrief. Options like a buffet line or a "build your own sandwich line" take too long.
- ▶ Afternoon snack: Something like popcorn or cookies can be a welcome treat in an all-day exercise.
- ▶ Throughout the day: Ensure plenty of water and fresh coffee is on hand all day long.

The more tranquil we become, the greater our success, our influence, our power for good. Calmness of mind is one of the beautiful jewels of wisdom.
— **James Allen,** *1864-1912*

Document preparation

EMSS prepares a "Document Summary" for every exercise we design. It is a simple one-page list of every document that was created for the exerise, simple printing instructions, who gets it, and the most current file name and number. It is your one one-stop guide for what needs to be reproduced and distributed.

Document summary

Here is a sample of a doc summary for an Advanced Tabletop.

ITEMS NEEDED	PRINTING INSTRUCTIONS	STATUS	# OF COPIES	WHO RECEIVES IT
Exercise agenda	n/a	Done V1R8_20151113	n/a	Do not print Can be sent to the team in advance as a "hold the date" notice.
Exercise plan	Colored ink on white paper, duplex	Done V1R13_20151113	43	Everyone
Exercise injects, master set	Colored ink on white paper, do not duplex	Done V1R16_20151120	9	Sim Team, Facilitator

ITEMS NEEDED	PRINTING INSTRUCTIONS	STATUS	# OF COPIES	WHO RECEIVES IT
Exercise injects, Message Center forms	Colored ink on white paper, do not duplex	Done V1R16_20151120	1	Facilitator
Tweets	Colored ink on white paper, do not duplex	Done V1R16_20151120	1	Facilitator
Radio broadcast	n/a	Done V1R3_20151110	n/a	Facilitator will bring on laptop; will need speakers to play recording.
Participant evaluation	B/W	Done V1R2_20151028	42	Everyone except Facilitator
Observer form	B/W	Done V1R1_20151027	4	All Observers
Sign-in sheet	B/W	In process V1R3_20151120	1	At entrance to exercise
Workshop Slide deck	n/a	Done V1R3_20151110	n/a	Will be displayed.

"Everyone" = All participants plus Facilitator

Pre-exercise training

The day or two before the exercise is a good time to do any of the required training that is necessary for everyone involved in the exercise – players, Simulators, Observers, and assistants. The good news is that most organizations rarely have real activations, but that means that the bad news is that they don't remember their roles. A double-edged sword! If you want the exercise to run smoothly and have your best chance for everyone to get the most out of the experience, some advance training of all involved can bring them up to a "level playing field" from the start of the exercise.

There are several trainings that you might need to conduct for the following audiences:
- ▶ Simulation Team
- ▶ Observers
- ▶ Exercise Assistants
- ▶ Exercise players

Simulation Team / Observers / Exercise Assistants

This orientation training is discussed in the Chapter 10. It is critical that all members of the exercise team know their individual roles and the responsibilities of that role, and are reasonably comfortable with them from the start.

Exercise Player training

The players themselves often benefit from training a few days before the exercise. At this point, on the verge of an exercise, they are usually highly receptive to the information. By having a quick refresher before the exercise, it is more likely they will "hit the ground running" and make greater strides in the exercise than if they had no training. Here are some subjects that we find appropriate with many of our clients:

Basic overview of the response team, including roles and responsibilities.

- ▶ How incidents are assessed, how to develop an incident action plan (IAP) and how to run an IAP meeting.
- ▶ How the command center and team operates.
- ▶ How calls are answered, logged, and tracked.
- ▶ Review of all forms they will encounter through the exercise.
- ▶ Outline of the documentation to be included on status boards.
- ▶ Overview of reports and briefings that may occur during the exercise.

Exercise Player reminders

This is a good time to reconnect with the exercise players. There may have been a relatively long gap between the "save the date" email and the actual exercise day. Now is when they should really be paying attention to your emails and missives. What "memory jogs" should you give them? What needs prompting at this point?

- ▶ It is always good to remind all participants about the agenda, goals, and objectives of the exercise. This will help them focus on the tasks at hand in advance and possibly prompt them to do some preparation. (If you haven't created a separate document with just these sections, simply take your exercise plan and delete everything except the agenda, goals, and objectives.)

- ▶ If you need them to bring something specific with them, this is the time to ask/remind them of what they should have with them or have immediate access to – anything they might need in order to do their assigned task. This could include such items as laptops, individual BCP documents, floor plans, mobile phones, chargers and power cords, maps, and other important and relevant pieces of equipment or information.

Your personal preparation

I have saved the most important thing for last. One thing I want you to keep in mind is that you hold the vision for this exercise. Yes, **YOU**.

You know the goals and objectives, the narrative, the flow of injects – and you are crystal clear about the silly little question, *"Why are we doing this?"* I can't emphasize how important that is. This deep, crystal clear vision will keep you on track, focused, and solid as a rock as the exercise unfolds.

Here's a short list of things you may want to review ***one more time:***
- ▶ Recheck the flow of the day, the narrative, the agenda, and the key injects.
- ▶ Reconfirm all of the logistics, including meeting room set-up, A/V and catering.
- ▶ Ensure that all materials have been printed and are correct (e.g., pages in the right order and oriented the same way and the correct documents ready to be given to the correct people).
- ▶ Go to bed early the night before and get a good night's sleep.
- ▶ Lastly, get up a little earlier than usual – then sit quietly and just visualize how it will go. Imagine it going as perfectly as planned and everyone engaged in the experince. I know that sounds crazy but visualization has been taught and has worked for Olympic athletes and high performers for years [30] – why not you, and why not now?

---

[30] "Olympians Use Imagery as Mental Training", NYT, February 22, 2014 http://www.nytimes.com/2014/02/23/sports/olympics/olympians-use-imagery-as-mental-training.html

Never again clutter your days or nights with so many menial and unimportant things that you have no time to accept a real challenge when it comes along. This applies to play as well as work. A day merely survived is no cause for celebration. You are not here to fritter away your precious hours when you have the ability to accomplish so much by making a slight change in your routine. No more busy work. No more hiding from success. Leave time, leave space, to grow. Now. Now! Not tomorrow!

— **Og Mandino,** *1923-1996*

Summary

All of your careful design work and planning has paid off. The rooms are ready, documents are printed, teams are trained, and everything is in place. You are at the starting line and poised for the gun to go off. The last thing is to make sure you are rested, holding the exercise vision in your mind, and visualizing success. It will be a great day!

CHAPTER 12

Game Day!

> ### *Chapter goals*
> 1. Review what to do before the exercise begins.
> 2. Check the list of "who" is doing "what" with everyone so there is no last-minute confusion.
> 3. Learn what makes a solid exercise briefing.
> 4. Look over the mechanics of observing, managing, and "righting" an exercise.
> 5. Play out in your mind the debrief and final steps once the exercise concludes.

Planning your time on Game Day

A few hours before the start

After all of your great planning, care, and preparation you are now ready to go!

- ▶ Plan to arrive at the exercise site **at least** one hour before the first agenda item is due to start. Again, this gives you the luxury of time to check and double-check that everything is in order and fix any problems that you missed earlier.
- ▶ For larger exercises, if at all possible, plan on having an assistant present who can be a resource for you.
- ▶ Make sure you have multiple ways of being reached during the exercise. At a minimum, this should include a reliable mobile phone with a fully-charged battery, and landline numbers that you will be near.
- ▶ Make sure all of the exercise team (Simulators and Observers) have checked in. If anyone has not shown up, and you are short a number of bodies, be prepared to punt and go to "Plan B."

"Plan B"
- **If Observers don't show up:**
  - Call others in to help. This works well for an Observer's role in particular, as the training can be quick.
  - Have Observers double-up on the teams that they are tasked with watching.
- **If Simulation Team members don't show up:**
  - Have the rest of the Simulation Team do double-duty. Spread out the injects among those who are there.
  - Delete the less important injects.
  - Combine several injects together.
  - Remind the rest of the Simulation Team to make sure that the phone gets answered.

Do you know what my favorite part of the game is?
The opportunity to play.
— Mike Singletary

Who's doing what? Exercise Team tasks on Game Day

Who is doing what on the exercise day? Here's a quick checklist to keep everyone focused:

Exercise Assistant
- Makes sure the room clocks are set to exercise time (if the exercise time is different from the "real time").
- Checks in with facilitator frequently.
- Plays any media as needed: video, radio broadcast, etc.
- Hand out any pertinent documents when directed or per a pre-established schedule.
- Keeps notes during the debriefing.
- Helps the facilitator with other tasks that will undoubtedly crop up.

Simulation Team

The Simulation Team is the engine that drives the exercise. It is now up to them to deliver. The Simulation Team should:
- ▶ Deliver injects on time.
- ▶ Be efficient when delivering injects. You want the delivery to be concise and to-the-point. (Remind them to keep their calls as short as feasibly possible to avoid players getting a busy signal.)
- ▶ Follow up on calls not being returned or issues not being addressed.
- ▶ Keep all fellow Simulation Team members and the Simulation Team Coordinator informed of any issues or potential problems.
- ▶ Use a status board in the Simulation Team room to note big issues that arise in the exercise.

Observers

Observers represent another set of eyes and ears for you. They help to keep the Facilitator and Simulation Team informed of what they are hearing and seeing around the exercise. The two most important activities of an Observer are to listen and follow the injects and the players. They also:
- ▶ Keep the facilitator informed of what's going on.
- ▶ Log notes on the Observer form.
- ▶ Look for teachable moments. (If a player gets stuck and the Observer can ask a reflective question to unstick them, let them do it. For example, if a player can be helped by reaching out to another player, a reflective question might sound like, "Have you checked in with Information Security about that issue?" Sometimes such a simple comment can get the player back in the game.)

One man can be a crucial ingredient on a team, but one man cannot make a team.

— *Kareem Abdul-Jabbar*

Starting line – The exercise briefing

Exercise welcome and kickoff

Whenever possible, have a senior organization leader do the exercise welcome and kick-off. You want and need an executive to:
- ▶ Speak about the strategic importance of planning and the exercise
- ▶ Acknowledge the players for their time and commitment
- ▶ Emphasize that exercises are for learning and that mistakes are expected and applauded.

This type of positive and encouraging welcome sets up the exercise and the players for success.

Exercise plan briefing

After the welcome and kickoff, it's time to distribute the Exercise Plan to all players and review the *entire* document with them.
- ▶ Thoroughly review the players' instructions and the narrative. It is important that players clearly understand all the information before you begin. If the plan was distributed in advance, it is still important to review the document with them. Just because it was sent to them in advance doesn't mean that they read it, or fully understand it.
- ▶ I like to particularly focus on the fact that exercises are for learning, mistakes are expected and applauded, and there are no grades.
- ▶ Make sure they understand the role of the Simulation Team as this can be confusing for players if they haven't experienced it before.
  - \> Advanced Tabletop: Introduce the Simulators at the back of the room and remind the players that they are responding as the caller to all injects, and that they are playing the outside world. To help identify them, EMSS usually places signs in front of each Simulator with titles such as:
    - ○ Emergency Responders.
    - ○ All contractors and vendors.
    - ○ Media: traditional and social.
    - ○ Other broad areas as applicable for your narrative and injects such as "any vendor or contractor."

- And, of course, all Simulators are "Geniuses-of-all-trades" (and anyone else the exercise player needs them to be).
> Functional and Full-Scale exercises: Review the phone directory, how it is used, and the role of the Simulation Team. This is especially critical for the players if a Simulation Team is a new concept for them.
> If you discover that players are not clear once the exercise starts, pause the action and make a room-wide announcement to ensure that the Simulation Team and phone directory are being used correctly.

At the conclusion of the exercise briefing, I always like to give the participants five minutes to get in place and "ground" themselves before starting to deliver the injects.

Champions keep playing until they get it right.
— *Billie Jean King*

Ready, set, go...

If you are using an audio broadcast or video, it is helpful to start the exercise with one of those aids in order to impart realism and set the tone. This often marks the "emotional start" to the exercise.

As the Exercise Facilitator, once the exercise begins, you need to float. Don't get into active problem-solving if you can help it. Just like the old surfer saying, it is always better to "hang loose." When something comes up – and don't worry, something will – solve it quickly and then keep floating.

At this point, your real work is already done. You just need to float and monitor, and try to keep everyone on an even keel. Of course, you will probably want to keep your fingers crossed – and maybe get out the rabbit's foot, too!

Simulation Team reminders

As an Exercise Facilitator, in addition to reminding the teams of their responsibilities (see Chapter 10, Exercise Team), I like to check in with the

Simulation Team and remind them to:
- ▶ Relax and have fun. Stay loose and be flexible (but not *too* flexible; they still have a core responsibility to keep the injects flowing on schedule).
- ▶ Stay in role. Don't go too crazy. Remember: No Martian landings, please!
- ▶ Check with the Exercise Facilitator, Assistant, or Simulation Team Coordinator to see if they have any questions.

Observer reminders

Ensure that the Observer(s) are in position and remind them to:
- ▶ "Be a fly on the wall."
- ▶ Observe participants in the key roles. Listen in on conversations.
- ▶ In an Advanced Tabletop, Observers can hand out the injects to their team on the prescribed schedule.
- ▶ Look at situation boards and forms.
- ▶ Check reports.
- ▶ Attend briefings.
- ▶ Talk with participants as appropriate.
- ▶ Follow the "key" injects around the room as they come in to see how they are managed.
- ▶ Interact with exercise players if "teachable moments" occur.

Observing exercise action

During an exercise, injects are delivered to the players using a variety of methods. The players then assess the inject and develop a response to the problem or question it presents based on all available information and the overall situation status.

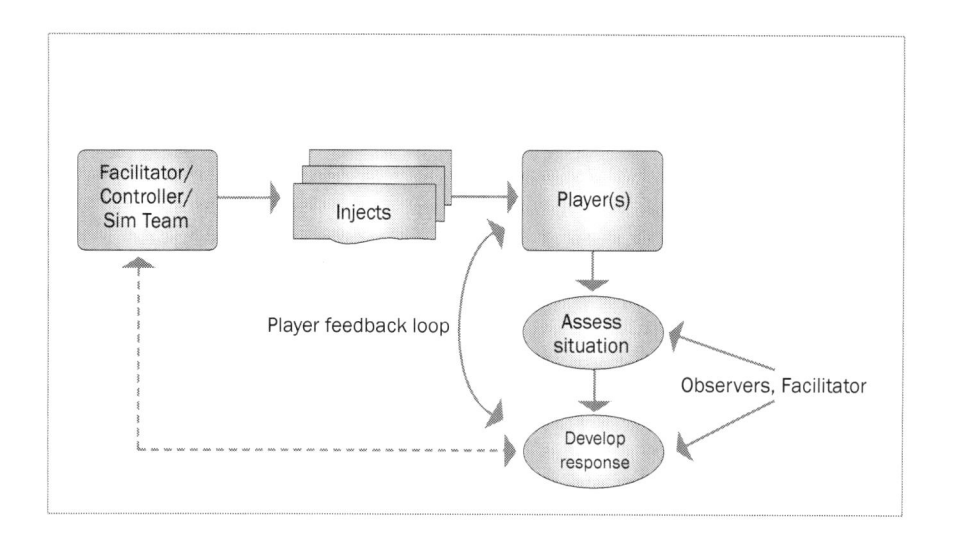

[Diagram: Facilitator/Controller/Sim Team → Injects → Player(s) → Assess situation → Develop response; Player feedback loop; Observers, Facilitator feeding into Assess situation and Develop response]

Mid-point check – Is everything okay?

Exercise pacing

As you were finalizing the inject document (see Chapter 8), the last thing you did was to sequence and time the injects over the course of the exercise "play time." Now that it's exercise day, when do you start delivering those injects? When do you stop? How do you adjust if the exercise seems like it's going too fast or too slow?

The question of when to start delivering injects depends on what your players normally do at the beginning of an exercise. If there is no assessment or planning activity, I generally start the injects ten minutes into the exercise. If you plan to start with an Incident Assessment and/or an Incident Action Planning session, then you have the option of starting the injects during that planning activity or after it has concluded. By and large, when I'm working with more experienced players, I will start delivering injects while the planning activity is going on. In your situation, you may want to give them a few minutes to "get their bearings."

Once the injects begin, be aware of how the participants are doing. Are they coping well? Overwhelmed? Underwhelmed? Although your injects are already timed, you can, of course, modulate the flow based on your observations. Too stressed? Slow it down a bit. Bored? Speed them up and encourage the Simulation Team to think of spontaneous injects that would keep those bored players engaged.

As the exercise unfolds, remember ***the*** critical exercise question, *"Why are we doing this exercise?"* In all likelihood, the answer is not "to overwhelm the participants." You will find that for the players, there is sometimes a fine line between their being bored and pulling their hair out. Both situations could have them wanting to run out of the room screaming. Make sure the injects are challenging for the players, but don't send them over the edge. Be on the alert for signs of obvious frustration among the players. If you overhear griping or complaining during the exercise, speak to them and see if you can resolve their concerns then and there (without doing anything to jeopardize the exercise goal and objectives, of course).

What are you doing while the Players are playing?

During the entire exercise, your task is to:
- ▶ Pay attention, observe, float.
- ▶ Observe player behavior.
- ▶ Eavesdrop on calls and conversations.
- ▶ Check in with Observers.
- ▶ Check in with the Simulation Team.
    - > If you (or an Observer) hear something that you think might "throw" the Simulation Team off, go tell them what is coming and help them with a response.
    - > Keep the Simulation Team posted on what is going on "out there" and possible ways to respond. They're in the Simulation room – you are their eyes and ears.
    - > Check their progress, help plot responses, or give encouragement.
- ▶ If it's possible, take lots of photos. These can be used post-exercise for articles and program education and promotion.
- ▶ Capture your observations in writing during the exercise. I always carry a notebook to capture comments, observations, and recommendations that I will be adding into the After-action Report. (Your smart phone may have the capability of capturing voice memos; you may find this more convenient and efficient if done

discreetly.) Even a short cryptic note will help you remember the thought when you sit down to write your report.

How to handle an exercise that's going "sideways"

An exercise going "sideways" is one that's drifting or going awry for one reason or another. There are a variety of ways that this can happen – sometimes players get hung up about an issue, they get stuck on a situation, or they simply hit the wall. Whatever the reason, you need to get it headed in the right direction again.

One of the ways to lessen this likelihood, is for you – as Facilitator – to constantly be in motion around the exercise – "floating" – listening, stepping in, and helping where appropriate. Constantly ask our basic question, "Why are we doing this exercise?" You want to challenge the team, but you do not want them to be needlessly frustrated. By walking around and observing the action, you can be on the lookout for situations that seem like they're headed the wrong way, conversations that don't seem to fit with the event, or signs of overactive imaginations.

Your job as a Facilitator is to assist and support the players and the exercise team where needed, with the goal of moving the exercise forward to meet the goals and objectives. Remember you are driving this experience to a success.

With those thoughts in mind, if you overhear something that you know is not true, was misconstrued, or otherwise doesn't fit with what you know about the exercise, you have a couple of options to fix it. Which you choose will depend on the exercise, the organization's culture, and the demeanor of the players. It is important, however, to step in and correct it at the moment:

- ▶ Point out the appropriate information on status boards, previous injects, or other places where the right information could be found. ("I can see on the status board that the power is still out on Main Street.")
- ▶ Ask the player to call the Simulation Team (as whichever entity would know the proper response) to verify the information. ("If you call the vendor, what is their schedule to deliver the new server?")
- ▶ Ask the Simulation Team to call in a correction to the player(s) who appear to be off-track. ("Just to confirm, it is a rumor that email is operating normally.")

Almost at the finish line

Whew! What likely took several months to plan is – quite amazingly – over in just a few hours. The phones have stopped ringing, the Simulation Team has delivered the last inject, the players have wrestled with their last request for "more laptops," the room has paper all over the place, and the exercise is now done. Hooray!

Well, hang on there, sports fans. Don't start celebrating yet, and certainly don't sit down to rest – you've still got things to do.

Exercise debrief

A critically important last piece still remains – the exercise debrief (or the "hotwash," as it's called in the public sector). The debrief sessions goals are to:
- ▶ Review and evaluate the exercise and the experience.
- ▶ Provide feedback regarding response plans and team performance.
- ▶ Identify and discuss lessons learned from the exercise.

This is an absolutely critical activity. It is important to make sure that you assign two people to take good notes as you facilitate the debrief. (It is exceedingly difficult to facilitate and scribe notes well at the same time.) The information you get from the debrief, combined with the written evaluations, your observations, and the comments from the Observers are a major portion of your After-Action Report. Besides providing valuable information for the exercise report, I often get many great gems from this session that feed into the next exercise.

Debrief format

During the debrief, you are trying to get participants' reactions to the day's events. The usual format I use for the debrief is to ask for impressions and observations from participants in the following order:
- ▶ Exercise players
- ▶ Team leaders, section chiefs, or business leaders
- ▶ Incident Commander or person in charge

Let everyone know the above sequence before you begin the debrief. That way, the participants understand the flow and if/when they may be called on specifically to respond. Especially inform team leaders or senior staff if they will be asked to share observations on behalf of their team so they can be prepared.

Debrief questions

I always ask just two basic questions. These questions provide a focus, while getting people to open up. Normally, they will probably get you 90% to 95% of the information you desire:
- ▶ "What worked in this experience?"
- ▶ "What needs improvement?"

Encourage all of the players to share their experiences and their key learnings. Move on to team leaders or business leaders (if using the Incident Command System, this would be section chiefs) and conclude with the Incident Commander (or person in charge of the incident).

The debriefing should be quick and move along at a good pace. Keep the exercise objectives in mind and, when possible, use them as a reference point.

Debrief style – "Game show host"

Not quite like Drew Carey on the "Price is Right," but I often do feel a bit like a game show host when I run the debrief this way. This style is expansive and inclusive. The Facilitator reviews the debrief basics, who speaks in what order, and then begins, drawing information out of the crowd by asking the first question and then waiting for the response.

I always start with the positive "What worked well in this exercise?" When that exploration has been exhausted, I move on to the "What needs improvement?" question (by the way, don't be surprised when people start mentioning items that fall into the other category as the discussion progresses – the responses are spontaneous, so not always organized by our neat little categories). As mentioned before, I suggest having at least two people to take notes, that way you are likely to capture all of the comments. I find that with two scribes, I am likely to get most of the comments; with one person, I only get about two-thirds and sometimes less. The scribing can be done by taking notes on an easel in front of the group, or by using regular notepads while seated.

Debrief style – Small groups

When the player population is quite large, it is often easier to use a small group format. In this style, the teams work together in their small groups to gather the same information. Have each team elect a scribe and a Facilitator (or assign the task to your Observer); the Facilitator will ask the two basic questions. When done, reassemble in the large group, where each team reports out on two to four of their top responses for both "what worked" and "what needs improvement."

Although this format saves time and can accommodate a large team, I find that I don't get as many varied responses when done this way.

Regardless of which style you select, be sure to collect all of the scribes' notes at the end for your After-action Report.

Written exercise evaluations

The last task of the day is to ask the participants to fill out the written evaluations. This is another crucial piece of feedback. Many people feel more comfortable sharing written thoughts anonymously than they do sharing out loud in a group, so I don't require names on written evaluations forms.

I encourage you to spend time developing this tool so that you get out of it what you want to know. It can provide great feedback to you on the status of your program, plans, teams, and issues – or it can tell you a whole lot of nothing if a question is ill-defined or not asked at all. (Evaluation documents are discussed in the Appendix.) Be sure to consider asking questions related to:
- ▶ Overall reaction to the exercise experience
- ▶ Adequacy of the existing plan
- ▶ Exercise itself
- ▶ Ideas for further training and exercises
- ▶ Suggestions for improvements to the exercise, training or plans

Two important words – "Thank you"

Before you call it a day and let the participants go, you need to say a big "thank you" to everyone who made this possible. The Exercise Team members (Simulation Team, Observers, Design Team members, Exercise Assistants) all need a big **THANK YOU** at the end. As the Facilitator, you definitely need to say this. Hopefully, a senior management person will echo this saying the final, important, "thank you" as well.

Push yourself again and again. Don't give an inch until the final buzzer sounds.
— *Larry Bird*

The cyber exercise effect

In all of my years of doing exercises, I have never seen an exercise that has an effect on participants like a cyber scenario. In most exercises, with even a very difficult narrative, the team will eventually get their arms around the problem and began to make headway and move forward towards a recovery strategy. Not so in a cyber exercise.

A vast majority of companies don't have plans about what they will do if they lose systems for any extended period of time and players are, frankly, shell-shocked. There is nothing in their business continuity plans to address this. It is likely that no department will have a plan. Executives are often humbled and struck by how overwhelming the whole experience is.

So don't be surprised if people hang around to talk or if the room is a little quieter than normal; or there isn't that "post-exercise high" that you may normally experience. As many players have said to me, a cyber incident is their greatest fear and the thing that they think is most likely to happen. In other words, it feels very, very real and very, very frightening.

The party's over!

Check in with your teams

Even though everyone will be going many directions after the exercise, before they leave, gather together your exercise team members (Simulation Team, Observers, Assistants) to capture some of their initial reactions to the exercise. They should have, of course, completed their own evaluations and observation documents, but it is great to get everyone together for a quick 20-minute check-in, and give some personal thank yous. They worked hard with you to make the day a big success. It's an ideal time to find out how it went from their perspective. They also might have some good ideas and suggestions for the development of the next exercise, or the program, the plan, or for team improvements.

Room clean-up

Be sure to allocate enough time and personnel to clean up the room properly.

- ▶ Determine what you want to save. Give clear instructions to your clean-up crew. Many documents can be used for writing the After-action Report; in some cases, the documents may be used for audit purposes.
- ▶ Don't forget things like:
    - > Message Center forms
    - > Status board sheets
    - > Staffing charts
    - > Incident Action Plans
    - > Written communications
    - > Call logs
    - > Sign-in sheets
- ▶ Collect all exercise materials (Exercise Plans, exercise injects, and any other exercise materials) and ensure that they are properly destroyed (shredding is recommended to avoid "bad" information from falling into the wrong hands).
- ▶ Ensure all equipment is returned and packed up for use the next time.

Collect all participant evaluations, observer forms, and sign-in sheets.

> *It ain't over 'til it's over.*
> *— Yogi Berra*

Exercise Team debrief

Lastly, we end this experience where we began – with your Exercise Team. Ideally, try to meet with the exercise Design Team no later than two weeks after the exercise (longer than this and memories start to fade). Going back full circle is a helpful experience as it allows you to really look at what happened in the exercise and compare it to what you expected. This meeting can be relatively short (an hour or less) and it can help you collect process improvement points, ideas and thoughts for your next exercise, along with program and plan development ideas.

> **Congratulations! You made it! Now you can celebrate!**

Summary

A cyber exercise – whether an Advanced Tabletop, Functional, or Full-Scale – will provide your team with a realistic experience of what could happen in a cyber incident. As such, it can be an invaluable tool for improving both individual, team, and organization performance in a situation that could otherwise severely disrupt the enterprise.

CHAPTER 13

Writing the after-action report

> *Chapter goals:*
> 1. Understand the purpose and importance of a well-crafted After-action Report (AAR).
> 2. Address the different components of an AAR.
> 3. Consider the importance of word choices and target audiences.
> 4. Learn how to use Standards and Guidelines in your AAR.

The After-action Report (AAR) is the formal documentation of the findings and learnings from the exercise. It is critically important to prepare this soon after the exercise in order to enjoy some of the "post-exercise bounce" that you will likely receive.

A cyber exercise often leaves people with what I call an "exercise hangover." They walk out of the room, and they don't have that great post-exercise feeling of "Wow, we managed through a tough situation and were able to get ahead of it!" Instead, they leave the room often feeling overwhelmed, depressed, and unsure of where to start in addressing the many issues that a cyber exercise raises. I have never seen this impact on any other narrative. The cyber exercise scenario often leaves people feeling a bit beleaguered.

The AAR can help give the players some direction to move forward, as well as help them place the experience in some context. It tells the story of the experience, captures the key learnings, and inspires people to take action.

What Is an after-action report?

The After-action Report is a formal record of the exercise. It is where you provide a complete summary of the experience. The AAR serves several important functions. It is where you will:

▶ Document exercise activities

- Identify key findings
- Develop a plan of action going forward

Document exercise activities

The AAR is the best tool you have for detailing what was actually exercised. This includes the:
- Narrative
- Players and departments
- Plans and processes

The AAR is the complete record of the exercise, which can be helpful for anyone who wants to know and understand how you conducted the exercise. Many entities are interested in this report. For example, the corporate audit risk committee, the risk department, your internal and external auditors, regulators – not to mention, Technology and Information Security departments, senior management, and the board of directors.

Identify key findings

The after-action report is also the best place to document your key findings – what worked and what needs improvement. Remember, one of the reasons exercises are done is to find out the things that don't work; and once those are identified, plot a course of corrective action. These findings need to be carefully articulated so that a plan may be developed.

Develop a plan of action going forward

How will the company fix the identified problems? What is the roadmap to resolve these issues? The AAR is where a plan of action for implementing improvements can be framed and detailed. Once an issue that needs improvement has been identified, make recommendations for those improvements, and suggest timelines and strategies to achieve the result.

Before you begin

Below are a few thoughts to consider before writing your report.

Your choice of words and language

Over the years, EMSS has made observations about the choice of words in our reports, in particular, the word "recommendation." Many of our clients are audited regularly by a variety of entities, including the Federal Financial Institutions Examination Council (FFIEC) and other outside entities, as well as internal auditors. The word "recommendation" carries a lot of weight with federal regulators and auditors. They often expect, if proposals or suggestions are made under "recommendations," that the organization must, in fact, do them. This often makes the audited enterprises feel like their hands are tied and pushes them to do something – even if it is not budgeted or is not the best time to make a change. For that reason, we frame our "recommendations" as "observations." They still are recommendations in our minds, but they are presented in a slightly different way.

The audience

The results of cyber exercises are of keen interest to a wide variety of individuals. You want your report to capture everything, but you don't necessarily want everyone to see everything. For that reason, EMSS is careful about how the report is formatted. We prepare two versions of the report:

- ▶ One version is the Exercise Report which includes the main body of the report (Executive Summary, Observations, and Facilitator Comments)
- ▶ The second version is the After-action Report which includes those first three sections and then the entire results of the exercise in the form of Appendices.

We split them that way for several reasons. The shorter version is perfect for executives, regulators, auditors, and/or others who want and need to see what was done but don't really need to see the entire exercise. The longer version contains verbatim comments from the debriefing session, observers, and participants which could be easily taken out of context by the casual reader or someone who was not present at the exercise. The longer version also includes verbatim incident action plans, communications, and other exercise deliverables. Lastly, it includes the complete exercise plan document. It is critically important to retain all of that detail, but not everyone needs or wants to see it.

Think carefully about the audience and how the information will be received before you start writing. As it will help you frame the structure and organization of the document.

Report format

Report components

EMSS structures its reports with two main components: the main body of the document, and the appendixes. As mentioned, the main body includes three basic sections:
1. Executive summary
2. Observations
3. Facilitator's comments

The appendices include other pertinent information:
- Debriefing summary
- Observer comments
- Participant evaluations
- Attendance and participant lists:
    - Exercise players lists
    - Exercise team
    - Design Team
    - Simulation Team
- Any specialized reports or information addendums (This could include copies of the Incident Action Plan(s), communications developed by a Communications Team, or written employee instructions)
- The exercise plan
- Exercise images

Main body of the report

Executive summary

The Executive Summary is a short section found on the first page or two of the document that recaps the longer report. The summary allows the reader to rapidly become familiar with the larger body of material without having to read all the detail. (Since the report is often distributed to many recipients, this summary may also be produced as a separate, short document. As a standalone document, this section can be an ideal recap for a meeting, audit committee, or Board report.)

The Executive Summary usually contains a brief statement of the exercise goals, a concise analysis of the exercise itself, and a summary of the exercise observations. One of the goals of the Executive Summary is to provide busy business executives and managers a concise overview of what was done and learned, and what the key exercise take-aways are. If they are interested in learning more, you can always provide them the entire AAR.

Observations

Many people are immediately drawn to this section, often with hope tinged with a bit of anxiety. Observations generally draw from four key areas:
- Exercise objectives
- National standards and guidelines
- Best practices
- Benchmarking within the industry

Exercise objectives

The fact the final report hinges on the objectives that you and your team set early on again emphasizes the importance of that process step and operating with well-crafted goals. You will use these objectives as a baseline to evaluate the exercise, and you will likely comment on observations and areas for improvement within those objectives.

National standards and/or guidelines

Standards and guidelines can help you frame the basis for your AAR, much like best practices. The field of cyber security is quickly morphing and changing as the threat landscape does. There are two documents that might inform your report and comments.
- ***ISO 22301:2012, Societal security – Business Continuity Management Systems***[31] This standard provides a framework to plan, establish, implement, operate, monitor, review, maintain, and continually

---
31 "Business continuity - ISO 22301 When things go seriously wrong" http://www.iso.org/iso/news.htm?refid=Ref1602

improve a business continuity management system.
- ***Framework for Improving Critical Infrastructure Cybersecurity, Version 1.0***[32] The Framework focuses on using business drivers to guide cybersecurity activities and consider cybersecurity risks as part of the organization's risk management processes. The Framework consists of three parts: the Framework Core, the Framework Profile, and the Framework Implementation Tiers.

Best practices

If there are best practices in the field of cyber security or continuity planning that can be used as a tool to improve the program or plan under review, point them out. Guide the reader towards considerations on how to incorporate the best practice into company procedures and processes.

Benchmarking within the industry

There may be key indicators within your industry that can be used to evaluate performance; if so, it is useful to use them for comparison. You might find these in:

- Published documents and journals
- Articles from professional organizations and societies
- National studies or white papers
- Professional association websites

Observations are always best received when they are straightforward, fact-based, and tied to industry-recognized practices or standards. This section often carries a lot of weight; because of that, they can be littered with political landmines. You will always need to keep that in mind when writing this section. You want people to hear what you have to say, but if all of their walls are up in defense, it is harder for them to do that. Whenever possible, footnote (or otherwise reference) practices, guidelines, or standards in this section as it will help build support for the observation.

As you are writing the observations, it is always good to remember that

---

32 "Framework for Improving Critical Infrastructure Cybersecurity", Version 1.0, National Institute of Standards and Technology, February 12, 2014, http://www.nist.gov/cyberframework/upload/cybersecurity-framework-021214.pdf

basic question, "Why were we doing this exercise?" As you are mulling that over, there are two other questions to keep in mind:
- ▶ What do you want these recommendations to do?
- ▶ Who is the audience for the report?

These two questions will also be helpful in developing the tone and style of the report.

When writing each recommendation, as when writing exercise goals, start each with an action-oriented verb for clarity. Use verbs such as "describe," "assess," "consider," "conduct," "initiate," "perform," "change," "incorporate," or "implement." Then go on to describe a clearly stated required action.

Sample cyber exercise recommendations
- ▶ *Develop in advance a set of template communications for a cyber incident across all platforms for initial basic messaging to all identified key stakeholders.* A communications team should never be looking at a blank piece of paper when they are developing communications during an event. Basic templates for initial messages to all identified key stakeholders can be written and approved in advance, and then reviewed quickly (and adapted as needed) at the time of a disaster and issued promptly. This should include internal and external messages for all likely platforms/tools, such as SMS (i.e., 140-character messages), voice, email, and website.
- ▶ *Explore how to manage communications without email or website.* What strategies can be used to continue to communicate effectively if the website goes down and/or email isn't available? Much communication now happens using email. What if it is not available? Include the loss of key technology tools in the Crisis Communications Plan, and develop a plan to ensure that the company messages continue to get out to key stakeholders.
- ▶ *Add cyber security issues (in particular, the loss of the network) and possible solutions and workarounds to Crisis Communication and Business Continuity plans.* Most people think of cyber security as a technology problem. It certainly is that, but it is also much, much more. Cyber security issues must be included in the Crisis

Communications templates and business continuity plans. Business Continuity (BC) plans assume that some technology will be available. What if the network is down or applications have become unsafe, unstable, or unreliable? All BC plans should include a section on the extended loss of technology and possible work-arounds.

Facilitator comments

There are many things that the Facilitator will see and observe during the exercise. It is important to capture these comments and reflections and share them. There are a couple of drivers to decide what you report on and what you do not. Two considerations:

- Are we answering the basic question, *"Why are we doing this exercise?"*
- Are we addressing the exercise objectives, i.e., what we observed against the objectives?

When writing observations, they must be:

- Fact-based
- Clear
- Concise
- Tied back to standards, practices, and industry benchmarking when possible

Keep in mind that even if the team has made a lot of mistakes, the tone and the framing of the observations can still be positive and encouraging. I always like to remind readers and players that it is always better to have made these mistakes in an exercise (with the chance of correcting them) than to make them during a real cyber incident.

Report appendix

Debriefing comments

This section should detail the results of the debriefing session. Preface the section by recapping what questions were asked. We always ask just two simple questions of the exercise players, "What worked?" and "What didn't work?" (or "What needs improvement?").

Be sure to edit the comments sufficiently so that they make sense and have a reasonable flow to them; however, don't edit them so much that you take out the meaning or context. Lastly, if you have asked particular groups to make comments, call out those groups by name either within the body of the comment, or as a separate group section. For example, "The Operations Team noted that security must be added outside the EOC to check badges and keep non-authorized people out."

Observer comments

Observer comments are usually included in the AAR verbatim, with the following exception: If the comment is based on a personal issue or the tone is inappropriate, it may be edited, or even deleted. Some valid observations are best delivered to the appropriate people in person rather than in writing. Obviously, it is one thing to share an observation verbally and quite another to see it on a page in black and white.

Exercise plan

The plan is a historical record of what you actually did in the exercise and is a great background for the AAR. It also helps put everything into context for readers of the AAR who may not have been in attendance. It's not usually necessary to include injects in the AAR (although you might mention notable ones anecdotally), but be sure to save them – they come in very handy for future exercises.

Participant evaluations

It is often useful to be able to see exactly how the participants felt about the exercise by including the evaluations into the AAR. However, transcribing the participant evaluations can take a lot of time, especially for a large exercise. An electronic survey (such as Survey Monkey or Zoomerang) may speed up the process; however, the return rate is often quite a bit lower than with paper surveys. As with Observer comments, participant evaluation comments are usually presented verbatim with the same caveat – if a comment is based on a personal issue or the tone is inappropriate, it may be edited or deleted.

Special documents and reports

Any deliverable that was part of the exercise objectives is ideal to include in this section. We usually include all Incident Action Plans and written communications to all key stakeholders.

Attendance lists

Some organizations may need or want to have a permanent record of who actually attended the exercise. This can help to satisfy certain audit requirements. And in some organizations, it provides an additional incentive to attend. As part of the formal record, you might also wish to list of who was on the exercise Design Team and Simulation Team as well. Minimally, it's good recognition.

Exercise images

Taking photos during an exercise provides an excellent record of the event, as well as being another tool to promote the activity and the overall program. The photos can be used in company newsletters or websites promoting the program. They also provide a nice touch on the AAR cover page and within the report. Photographs can also be shared directly with participants and departments. Not coincidentally, photos recognize the people who made it happen. They will appreciate that.

Report editing

Once the report is complete, have at least one other person read it carefully. You are too close to it to catch errors, and you don't want to send it out without another set of eyes poring over the text, flow, grammar and spelling. If you are blessed to have someone in your group with good writing and editing skills, ask them to look it over. Just keep in mind that you shouldn't take suggestions or revisions personally; it's all about getting the best document and, therefore, the best results.

Summary

There is tremendous power in conducting exercises, but their value is limited if there is no documentation that they ever happened, or what could be done to better them. An After-action Report provides key feedback to everyone involved – not to mention the executive sponsors. It is an excellent return on the organization's investment.

CHAPTER 14

Now what? Exercise follow-up

Chapter goals
1. Get your AAR in front of the right people.
2. Understand the importance of having a plan of action.
3. Learn about post-exercise tracking and follow-up.
4. Reflect on the power of a well-crafted exercise.

Once the After-action Report is written, edited, and ready to be sent, you may be thinking that you can take a deep breath and sigh as you bask in the post-exercise glow. Finally done!

Not so fast.

Exercise follow-up is just as important, and in fact, some might argue that it is the most important part of the exercise job.

Here is a short list of what you should be planning and thinking about now:
- Getting the report in front of the right people.
- Gain consensus on a plan of action:
  > Plan revisions
  > Assignments
  > Required funding
- Tracking and follow-up
- Schedule the next exercise

Getting the report in front of the right people

In the past year, I have found that the topic of cyber security – and an organization's level of cyber preparedness – doesn't take a lot of pushing. From the board of directors and senior executives down, everyone wants to know if the company is ready. It won't be a challenge to get the report in front of the right people. On the contrary. However, they might not like what it has to say – and that's a totally different issue.

Acceptance of the report and recommendations by key individuals is likely to be tied to funding, staffing, and other key resources. Here is a possible list of the "right people" to consider when "shopping" your report around:

- ▶ Your corporate sponsor
- ▶ Senior management
- ▶ The board of directors
- ▶ Senior audit management
- ▶ Corporate Risk Committee

It is important that you have laid the proper foundation before sharing the report with any high-profile individuals or groups. The goal should be to eliminate anyone's being surprised or embarrassed. To achieve that, you first need to develop insights as to what might cause each person or group to be surprised or embarrassed. Beware: the answers may not be the same for them as they are for you. Misunderstanding this may cause *"you"* to be surprised or embarrassed.

I have found that whenever possible, it is ideal to have a face-to-face discussion of the key findings and observations. In some cases, I'd suggest it's crucial. Cyber incidents can be complicated, and it is helpful to see the audience's body language and ascertain how they are reacting to the report. Sometimes the report will point out findings that people don't want to hear. Keep it in mind. It's hard to always know all the political sensitivities. Tread lightly and stay observant.

I would highly recommend that you have the key individuals involved in the Technology Design Team present the actual attack scenario that was used in the exercise. Let them explain how it unfolded with all of the attack nuances. I have found this so helpful for executives, in particular. They get a fuller and deeper understanding of the cyber issues. (Remember that in the exercise, the attack scenario will never be disclosed, since in reality, it would take weeks or months to be known.)

Gain Consensus on a plan of action

Before you can develop a plan of action, ensure that those responsible for, and charged with, fixing the issues understand them. Educate those decision-

makers about the observations. Chart a course of action that results in the successful resolution of the observations. As part of this plan, you will need to develop the strategy for:
- Plan revisions
- Assignments
- Required funding

Tracking and follow-up

Once you have an agreed-upon plan of action, take time to chart all observations and action steps, including a timeline for completion. All deliverables need an owner and a completion date. Some may also include intermediate dates as "touch points." Don't forget to consider whether you have the resources that you need to achieve the plan-of-action. This includes people, applications, equipment, and other items. If you discover you have a shortfall, determine the possible work-arounds to still be successful.

Tracking

Tracking tools are important to chart progress towards achievement of the goals and program improvement. This could be a simple Excel spreadsheet or could be something more complex and sophisticated using a project management software. The critically important thing is to follow up. Follow-up is the key!

A tracking sheet doesn't have to be extensive; a simple format would include the following information:
- Task(s)
- Responsible party
- Due date
- Status
- Comments and follow-up

This step is absolutely essential to ensure that actions are completed. There will likely be a great deal of interest in the exercise findings and remediation. Executives will likely want to know your progress and expect regular reports.

Scheduling the next exercise

How do you know if your improvements made a difference and your revised plans have fixed the identified issues? Of course, you probably guessed the answer to this simple, rhetorical question: you can wait for a cyber incident and see how it goes, or you can do another exercise. As you already know, the latter is less stressful and generally has the best results!

Summary

We have now come full circle in the process of exercise design. As you can see, it begins and ends with an exercise. Exercises remain one of your most powerful tools to improve your organization's readiness for a cyber attack. Time is a-wastin'. Get started today!

Glossary

The terminology of Business Continuity and Crisis Management has, over the years, become fairly standardized, but the language around cyber threats is fairly new. This glossary is aimed at reducing any confusion while reading the book or engaged in exercise design

- **Advanced Persistent Threats (APT)** – An adversary that possesses sophisticated levels of expertise and significant resources which allow it to create opportunities to achieve its objectives by using multiple attack vectors (e.g., cyber, physical, and deception).
- **After-action Report (AAR)** – A summary of lessons learned from an exercise or an incident. The AAR also includes recommendations for improvements.
- **Attack** – An attempt to gain unauthorized access to system services, resources, or information or an attempt to compromise system integrity.
- **"Back door"** – Unauthorized hidden software or hardware mechanism used to circumvent security controls.
- **Business Continuity Plans (BCP)** – The documentation of a predetermined set of instructions or procedures that describe how an organization's mission/business functions will be sustained during and after a significant disruption.
- **Business Continuity exercise** – A mechanism to test the recovery of a mission-critical business process or business department.
- **Business Impact Analysis (BIA)** – The study of an enterprise's requirements, processes, and interdependencies used to characterize technology and business unit contingency requirements and priorities in the event of a significant disruption.

- **Crisis communications** – Factual messages and statements by an involved organization to its stakeholders in response to a crisis (incident, event).
- **Crisis Management Team (CMT)** – See "Incident Management Team."
- **Cyber attack** – A breach targeting an enterprise's use of cyberspace for the purpose of disrupting, disabling, destroying, or maliciously controlling a computing environment/infrastructure; or destroying the integrity of the data, or stealing controlled information. A term commonly used by the media.
- **Cyber incident** – Actions taken through the use of computer networks that result in an actual or potentially adverse effect on an information system and/or the information residing in that system.
- **Cyber security** – The ability to protect or defend the use of cyberspace from cyber attacks.
- **Denial of Service (DoS)** – The prevention of authorized access to resources or the delaying of time-critical operations. (Time-critical may be milliseconds or it may be hours depending upon the service provided.)
- **Disaster Recovery (DR) exercise** – A mechanism to test the technology recovery aspects of a plan.
- **Disaster Recovery Plan (DRP)** – A written plan for recovering one or more information systems at an alternate facility in response to a major hardware or software failure or destruction of facilities.
- **Drill** – A supervised field response activity with a limited focus to test a particular procedure. Drills usually highlight and closely examine a limited portion of the overall emergency response plan.
- **Emergency incident** – An event or occurrence that 1) requires an immediate response to bring the situation under control and restore normality, and 2) can threaten the health or safety of those involved, responders, and people in the surrounding area.
- **Emergency management** – The organization and management of resources and responsibilities for dealing with all aspects of emergencies, including mitigation, preparedness, response, and recovery.
- **Emergency Operations Center (EOC)** – An established location/facility at which selected management can receive information pertaining to an incident and from which they can provide direction, coordination, and support to emergency operations.

- **Emergency Response exercise** – A mechanism to test the ability of an Incident Management Team to handle a defined event according to the response aspects of a plan.
- **Emergency Response Plan** – An Emergency Response Plan that establishes an organizational structure and procedures for response to life safety emergencies.
- **Exercise Design Team** – A group of individuals who are tasked with assisting in the design of the exercise. These individuals are commonly subject matter experts from the organization. Their role includes validating the exercise narrative and developing the exercise injects.
- **Exercise Facilitator/Director** – The individual in charge of the exercise from design through the delivery of the exercise. He or she may also be the author of the After-action Report.
- **Exercise injects** – Information that is inserted or "injected" into the in-progress exercise that expands the story, provides information, asks a question, and/or requires the exercise players to "do something."
- **Exercise plan** – A document outlining the complete background of the exercise, including the narrative. The exercise plan provides all of the necessary background information for the players to begin the exercise. Sometimes called the "players' book."
- **Exercise players** – All participants in the exercise who are responsible for responding to the event.
- **Exercise script** – The text of the exercise injects.
- **Exercise team** – The entire team of individuals who are involved in the management of the exercise. This includes the exercise facilitator/director, exercise Design Team, Simulation Team, Evaluator, Controller, and Observers, but not the players.
- **Firewall** – A hardware/software capability that limits access between networks and/or systems in accordance with a specific security policy.
- **Forensics** – The practice of gathering, retaining, and analyzing data and the techniques to preserve evidence from a particular computing device in a way that is suitable for presentation in a court of law.
- **Full-scale exercise** – A mechanism to test the mobilization of all (or as many as possible) of the response components. A full-scale exercise takes place in "real time," employs real equipment, and tests several

emergency functions.
- **Functional exercise** – A mechanism to simulate a disaster in the most realistic manner possible without moving the people or equipment to a real site. A functional exercise utilizes a carefully designed and scripted scenario with timed messages and communications between simulators and players.
- **Goal** – A broad statement of the reason the exercise is being conducted. The goal explains what is being assessed or evaluated.
- **Hacker** – An unauthorized user who gains, or attempts to gain, access to an information system.
- **Homeland Security Exercise and Evaluation Program (HSEEP)** – A capabilities and performance-based exercise program that provides a standardized methodology and terminology for exercise design, development, conduct, evaluation, and improvement planning used in the United States.
- **Identification** – The process of verifying the identity of a user, process, or device – usually as a prerequisite for granting access to resources in an IT system.
- **Incident** – A violation or imminent threat of violation of computer security policies, acceptable use policies, or standard security practices.
- **Incident Action Plan (IAP)** – A document that contains objectives reflecting the overall incident strategy and specific tactical actions and supporting information for the next operational period on an incident.
- **Incident Command System (ICS)** – A systematic process used for the command, control, and coordination of response and recovery operations. ICS allows organizations to work together using common terminology and operating procedures to control personnel, facilities, equipment, and communications at a single incident scene. It facilitates a consistent response to any incident by employing a common organizational structure that can be expanded and contracted based on the level of required response.
- **Incident Management Team (IMT)** – The tactical team in charge of managing an incident from response through recovery.
- **Incident Response Plan** – The documentation of a predetermined set of instructions or procedures to detect, respond to, and limit consequenc-

es of a malicious cyber attacks against an organization's information system(s).
- **Initial Assessment Team (IAT)** – The team responsible for evaluating incidents, assigning an incident level, and determining if plans should be activated.
- **Insider threat** – An entity with authorized access (i.e., within the security domain) that has the potential to harm an information system or enterprise through destruction, disclosure, modification of data, and/or denial of service.
- **Internet** – The single, interconnected, worldwide system of commercial, governmental, educational, and other computer networks that share (a) the protocol suite specified by the Internet Architecture Board (IAB), and (b) the name and address spaces managed by the Internet Corporation for Assigned Names and Numbers (ICANN).
- **Intranet** – A private network employed within the confines of a given enterprise (e.g., internal to a business or agency).
- **Intrusion detection system** – Hardware or software product that gathers and analyzes information from various areas within a computer or a network to identify possible security breaches, which include both intrusions (attacks from outside the organizations) and misuse (attacks from within the organizations.).
- **Joint Information Center (JIC)** – A central location where personnel with public information responsibilities perform critical emergency information functions, crisis communications, and public affairs functions.
- **Key injects** – Designated injects that will be tracked from the time they are delivered into the exercise through their successful management/conclusion. Key injects are tracked by evaluators and/or controllers in the exercise who work closely with the Simulation Team to ensure that the event is properly managed.
- **Malicious code** – Software or firmware intended to perform an unauthorized process that will have adverse impact on the confidentiality, integrity, or availability of an information system. A virus, worm, Trojan horse, or other code-based entity that infects a host.
- **Malware** – A program that is inserted into a system, usually covertly, with the intent of compromising the confidentiality, integrity, or avail-

ability of the victim's data, applications, or operating system or otherwise annoying or disrupting the victim.
- **Master Scenario Events List (MSEL)** – A chronologically-sequenced outline of the simulated events and key event descriptions that participants will be asked to respond to during the course of exercise play.
- **Maximum Tolerable Downtime** – The amount of time mission/business processes can be disrupted without causing significant harm to the organization's mission.
- **National Incident Management System (NIMS)** – A system mandated by Homeland Security Presidential Directive 5 that provides a consistent nationwide approach for governments, the private sector, and non-governmental organizations, to work effectively and efficiently together to prepare for, respond to, and recover from domestic incidents, regardless of cause, size, or complexity.
- **Network** – Information system(s) implemented with a collection of interconnected components. Such components may include routers, hubs, cabling, telecommunications controllers, key distribution centers, and technical control devices.
- **Objectives** – The specific activities and deliverables that will be required in an exercise.
- **Observers** – Persons who, during an exercise, are assigned to teams or groups specifically to assess the activities that they observe. Their evaluation is made against the exercise objectives. Observers are sometimes referred to as evaluators.
- **Operational Period** – The period of time scheduled for execution of a given set of operation actions as specified in the Incident Action Plan. Operational Periods can be of various lengths, although usually not over 24 hours.
- **Orientation exercise** – A mechanism to test a response team that uses a simple narrative. It is often delivered by a PowerPoint slide presentation in a conversational, non-threatening manner. It is often used to orient a team to a plan.
- **"Parking lot"** – A flip chart or whiteboard that will be used to capture any questions or issues that come up during the exercise or training but can't be addressed at that time. The usual practice is to revisit any "park-

ing lot" issues at the end of the allotted time and make a plan for addressing any unresolved questions or issues then.
- **Participant instructions** – Informs the exercise players of what they can expect from the exercise and what is expected of them during the exercise.
- **Phishing** – Tricking individuals into disclosing sensitive personal information through deceptive computer-based means.
- **Precursor** – A sign that an attacker may be preparing to cause an incident.
- **Preparedness** – The wide range of deliberate, critical tasks and activities necessary to build, sustain, and improve the operational capability to prevent, protect against, respond to, and recover from domestic incidents.
- **"Players' book"** – See "Exercise plan."
- **Recovery Point Objective (RPO)** – The point in time to which data must be recovered after an outage.
- **Recovery Time Objective (RTO)** – The overall length of time an information system's components can be in a recovery phase before negatively impacting the organization's mission or mission/business functions.
- **Remediation** – The act of correcting a vulnerability or eliminating a threat, for example installing a patch, adjusting configuration settings, or uninstalling a software application.
- **Remote access** – Entrance to an organizational information system by a user (or an information system acting on behalf of a user) communicating through an external network (e.g., the Internet).
- **Resilience** – The ability to quickly adapt and recover from any known or unknown changes to the environment through holistic implementation of risk management, contingencies, and continuity planning.
- **Rogue device** – An unauthorized node on a network.
- **Security controls** – The management, operational, and technical controls (i.e., safeguards or countermeasures) prescribed for an information system to protect the confidentiality, integrity, and availability of the system and its information.
- **Simulation** – Simulation is the imitation of the operation of a real-world process or system over time. Something that is made to look, feel, or behave like something else especially so that it can be studied or used to train people.

- **Spam** – The abuse of electronic messaging systems to indiscriminately send unsolicited bulk messages.
- **Spoofing** – Faking the sending address of a transmission to gain illegal entry into a secure system, for example by impersonating, masquerading, piggybacking, or mimicking a different entity.
- **Spyware** – Software that is secretly or surreptitiously installed into an information system to gather information on individuals or organizations without their knowledge; a type of malicious code.
- **Tabletop exercise, Advanced** – Same as a Basic Tabletop, with the addition of a Simulation Team present in the exercise room.
- **Tabletop exercise, Basic** – A process to test an organization's emergency management plan and procedures and to highlight issues of coordination and assignment of responsibilities. Basic Tabletop exercises use written and verbal scenarios to evaluate the effectiveness of the team. Tabletop exercises do not physically simulate specific events, nor do they utilize equipment or deploy resources.
- **"Teachable moments"** – An unplanned opportunity that arises in the exercise where a facilitator/controller/evaluator has an ideal chance to offer insight to his or her players. It is a fleeting opportunity that must be sensed and seized.
- **Threat** – Any circumstance or event with the potential to adversely impact organizational operations (including mission, functions or reputation), organizational assets, individuals, other organizations, or the nation through an information system via unauthorized access, destruction, disclosure, modification of information, and/or denial of service.
- **Threat scenario** – A set of discrete threat events, associated with a specific threat source or multiple threat sources, partially ordered in time.
- **Trojan horse** – A computer program that appears to have a useful function but also has a hidden and potentially malicious function that evades security mechanisms — sometimes by exploiting legitimate authorizations of a system entity that invokes the program.
- **Unauthorized access** – When a user, legitimate or not, accesses a resource that the user is not permitted to use.
- **Virus** – A computer program that can copy itself and infect a computer without permission or knowledge of the user. A virus might corrupt or

delete data on a computer, use email programs to spread itself to other computers, or even erase everything on a hard disk.
- **Vulnerability** – Weakness in an information system, system security procedures, internal controls, or implementation that could be exploited or triggered by a threat source.
- **Worm** – A self-replicating, self-propagating, self-contained program that uses networking mechanisms to spread itself. See "malicious code."
- **"Zombie"** – A program that is installed on one system to cause it to attack other systems.

A great resource for information security terms is available from the National Institute of Standards and Technology NIST: Glossary of Key Information Security Terms, June 05, 2013 http://www.nist.gov/customcf/get_pdf.cfm?pub_id=913810

Appendix —
Exercise checklists and sample forms

Chapter goals:
1. Review all of the activities necessary to conduct:
   - An advanced tabletop exercise
   - A functional and full-scale exercise
2. Show the different types of forms necessary for most exercises.

Exercise checklists

Here are two very helpful checklists: one for an advanced tabletop and the other for a functional or full-scale exercise. Think of these as mini-project plans. We strongly recommend that you start here and spend some serious time to develop the checklist or your own project plan to help you stay on track and focused during the design process. There is a lot to do and it is very easy to get distracted and begin to miss deadlines.

Advanced tabletop exercise checklist

This checklist can be used as a guide and timeline for developing an Advanced Tabletop Exercises.

ADVANCED TABLETOP EXERCISE CHECKLIST		
ACTIVITY	**DATE**	**ASSIGNED TO**
20 weeks before		
☐ Select date and time for exercise.		
☐ Reserve room.		
☐ Send out a "save the date" communication (email, voicemail, fax, etc.) to the players.		
☐ Explore the question, *"why are we doing this exercise?"* (See Chapter 7.)		

ADVANCED TABLETOP EXERCISE CHECKLIST		
ACTIVITY	**DATE**	**ASSIGNED TO**
☐ Develop list of likely Exercise Design Team members, both IT and business units.		
☐ Ask all Design Team members to serve as Simulators on the day of the exercise.		
19 weeks before		
☐ Develop the goal and objectives of the exercise.		
☐ Validate goal and objectives with appropriate individuals; modify accordingly.		
☐ Develop basic exercise narrative.		
☐ Develop complete Exercise Plan.		
☐ Develop Document Summary form.		
☐ Select dates for three IT Design Team meetings		
☐ Send out email invite to IT Design team members.		
18 to 16 weeks before		
☐ Conduct three IT Design Team meetings and complete the IT narrative timeline.		
☐ Send out email invites to Business Unit Design Team members.		
15 weeks before		
☐ Do any refinement necessary on the IT timeline narrative and get ready for the Business Unit Design Team meetings.		
13 weeks before		
☐ Hold Business Unit Design Team meeting number 1. Review Exercise Plan and narrative. Discuss exercise injects. Issue homework assignment for injects (due in 7 days).		
12 weeks before		
☐ Review homework, revise, tweak, and send back full inject list along with any Exercise Plan revisions to the team.		
11 weeks before		
☐ Hold Business Unit Design Team meeting number 2. Review all injects. Evaluate status. Decide if the team needs more homework and if you need meeting number 3. If necessary, issue second homework assignment.		

ADVANCED TABLETOP EXERCISE CHECKLIST		
ACTIVITY	DATE	ASSIGNED TO
10 weeks before		
☐ Review homework, tweak, revise, and send back full inject list, along with any Exercise Plan revisions to the team.		
☐ Write radio/video broadcast(s) scripts.		
9 weeks before		
☐ Hold Business Unit Design Team meeting number 3. Review all injects and finalize.		
☐ Record radio or video broadcast(s).		
8 weeks before		
☐ Send exercise agenda to players. Include goal, objectives, and agenda/timeline.		
☐ If you are using slides, prepare a slide deck.		
☐ Develop participant evaluation.		
3 weeks before		
☐ Order audio-visual equipment (LCD projector, flip charts, etc.).		
2 weeks before		
☐ Order catering for exercise (coffee, lunch, etc.). If ordering lunch, consider a box lunch; this makes the food serving go much faster.		
☐ Determine how to play the radio/video broadcast. Do any necessary troubleshooting.		
1 week before		
☐ Order printed materials (Exercise Plan, Evaluations, other documents as necessary).		
☐ Send follow-up email to players reminding them of the exercise. Include reminder of any items they may need to bring.		
☐ Provide training to Simulators on how to be a Simulator. Review likely responses and role play.		
1 day before exercise		
☐ Set up room.		
☐ Check proper functioning of all audio-visual equipment.		
☐ Test radio broadcast to ensure it plays with no issues.		

ADVANCED TABLETOP EXERCISE CHECKLIST		
ACTIVITY	**DATE**	**ASSIGNED TO**
☐ Set up "parking lots" (flip charts or whiteboards that will be used to capture any questions or issues that come up during the training but can't be addressed at that time).		
Exercise day		
☐ Conduct exercise.		
☐ Be brilliant!		
☐ Collect participant evaluations at the end.		
☐ Collect and save and/or properly destroy exercise materials after the exercise.		
No longer than 2 weeks AFTER exercise		
☐ Write After-action Report (AAR).		
☐ Distribute AAR.		

For every minute spent organizing, an hour is earned.

— *Benjamin Franklin*

Functional or full-scale exercise checklist

This checklist can be used as a guide and timeline for developing a Functional or Full-scale exercise. The primary difference between a Functional and Full-Scale exercise is time. It will generally take at least 8 more weeks to design a Full-Scale exercise, and you must deal with the logistics of planning for an exercise at an alternate site and/or other field response activities.

FUNCTIONAL OR FULL-SCALE EXERCISE CHECKLIST		
ACTIVITY	DATE	ASSIGNED TO
24 weeks before		
☐ Select date and time for exercise.		
☐ Reserve exercise room.		
☐ Send out a "save the date" communication (email, voicemail, fax, etc.) to the players.		
☐ Explore the question, Why are we doing this exercise? *(See Chapter 7.)*		
☐ Develop list of likely Exercise Design Team members. ☐ Ask all Exercise Design Team members to serve as Simulators on the day of the exercise.		
23 weeks before		
☐ Develop the goal(s) and objectives of the exercise.		
☐ Validate goal(s) and objectives with appropriate individuals; modify accordingly.		
☐ Develop exercise narrative.		
☐ Develop complete Exercise Plan.		
☐ Develop Document Summary form.		
☐ Select dates for 3 to 5 Design Team meetings.		
☐ Send out email invite to IT Design Team members.		
22 to 18 weeks before		
☐ Conduct IT Design Team meetings and complete the IT narrative timeline.		
17 weeks before		
☐ Send out email invite to Business Unit Design Team members.		
16 to 8 weeks before		
☐ Begin Business Unit Design Team meetings.		
☐ Develop Business Unit narrative.		

FUNCTIONAL OR FULL-SCALE EXERCISE CHECKLIST

ACTIVITY	DATE	ASSIGNED TO
☐ Review homework, revise, tweak and send back full inject list along with any Exercise Plan revisions to the team.		
6 weeks before		
☐ Write radio/video broadcast(s) scripts.		
5 weeks before		
☐ Record radio/video broadcast(s).		
4 weeks before		
☐ Send exercise agenda to players. Include goal, objectives, and agenda/timeline.		
☐ Develop Simulation Team evaluation.		
☐ Develop participant evaluation.		
☐ Develop controller/evaluator/observer form.		
☐ Develop phone directory 'shell' (entries with no phone numbers).		
3 weeks before		
☐ Order audio-visual equipment (LCD projector, flip charts, etc).		
2 weeks before		
☐ Order catering for exercise (coffee, lunch, etc.). If ordering lunch, try consider a box lunch; this makes the food serving go much faster.		
☐ Determine how to play the radio broadcast. Do any necessary troubleshooting.		
☐ Prepare Executive Briefing document.		
☐ Confirm which of your Design Team will be your Simulators. If there are too many, some can become observers; if you have too few, start lining up others.		
1 week before		
☐ Order printed materials (Exercise plan, Evaluations, other documents as necessary).		
☐ Send follow-up email to players reminding them of the exercise. Include reminder of any items they may need to bring.		
☐ Provide training to Simulators (Design Team volunteers or others) on how to be a Simulator. Review likely responses and role play.		
☐ Provide training to Evaluators/ Controllers/ Observers.		

FUNCTIONAL OR FULL-SCALE EXERCISE CHECKLIST		
ACTIVITY	**DATE**	**ASSIGNED TO**
2 days before exercise		
☐ Add phone numbers to the phone directory. . This is done close to the exercise date to avoid last minute changes and the possibility of an incorrect directory.		
Day before exercise		
☐ Set up room.		
☐ Check phone lines.		
☐ Verify proper functioning of all audio-visual equipment.		
☐ Play radio broadcast to ensure it plays with no issues.		
☐ Determine which room will be used for the press conference; if separate room than the exercise, set it up.		
☐ Set up Simulation Team room and check phones.		
☐ Set up "parking lots." (Flip charts or whiteboard used to capture any questions or issues that come up during the training but can't be addressed at that time.)		
☐ Conduct 30-minute exercise briefing for the executives. (If unable to do in person, then send executive briefing via email.)		
Exercise day		
☐ Conduct exercise.		
☐ Collect participant evaluations at the end.		
☐ Collect and properly destroy exercise materials after the exercise.		
No longer than 2 weeks after exercise		
☐ Write After-Action Report (AAR).		
☐ Distribute AAR.		

Three rules of work:
Out of clutter find simplicity; from discord find harmony;
in the middle of difficulty lies opportunity.

— *Albert Einstein*

Sample materials and forms

Here are a few sample communications and forms that we use for most of our exercises.

"Save the date" Communication

> Please save the date for our Cyber Exercise to be held on <<exercise date and time>> at <<company name>>. This exercise is critically important to ensure that our plans meet the challenge of a cyber incident, that we are all familiar with our planned responses, and we can execute them quickly and efficiently if necessary. You will be playing an important role and your attendance at this significant exercise is critical.
>
> ▶ Please mark your calendar for <<date and time>>. The session will be held at the <<meeting location>>.
> ▶ Additional information will be sent a few weeks prior to the session. Please confirm your attendance.
> ▶ I look forward to seeing you on <<date>>

Don't forget to ask all players to send an RSVP back to you. Silence does not equal affirmation. If you get no response, follow up.

Document summary

This is one of the ways EMSS keeps exercise documents organized. The Doc Summary lists all items being produced for the exercise. You may also find it helpful to indicate how many copies to make if the documents will be provided on paper.

EXERCISE DOCUMENT SUMMARY

DOCUMENTS PRODUCED	PRINTING INSTRUCTIONS	DEVELOPMENT STATUS	WHO RECEIVES IT	DATE COMPLETED
Exercise Agenda and "Save the Date" email	N/A – Send as an email to all exercise players		Everyone	
Exercise Plan	B/W		Everyone	
Exercise video	N/A – need LCD projector to display/audio		N/A	
Phone Directory	Print on colored paper		Everyone	
Evaluator Form	B/W		Evaluators	
Sim Team Evaluation	B/W		Sim Team	
Participant Evaluation	B/W		Everyone	
Executive Briefing	Sent as a PDF to the executives 24 hours in advance of exercise		Executives	

Agenda

The following is an example of a standard exercise agenda.

<<Company memo or document header>>
Cyber Exercise Agenda <<date>>

Goal
Assess ability of the <<name of team>> to develop the appropriate strategies to manage a cyber incident and continue business operations.

Objectives
- Assess the ability of the Incident Assessment Team to assess the incident and develop an initial response.
- Assess the ability of the Incident Commander to brief the Executive Leadership Team.
- Assess the ability of the Incident Commander (IC), and designated Team Leaders to conduct a timely Incident Action Planning (IAP) meeting and develop a written IAP.
- Incorporate the Information Security Team (IST) into the exercise, and assess communications between the IST and the <<name of team>>. Determine gaps or overlaps, and note areas for improvement.
- Assess the ability of the communications team to develop the <<company name>> message and produce the necessary communication materials for all key stakeholders.
- Assess the effectiveness of the emergency notification system (ENS) and its use during the exercise.

EXERCISE AGENDA		
ACTIVITY	**TIME**	**DISCUSSION LEADER**
Welcome and introductions, review exercise plan	8:00 AM – 8:30 AM	J. Smith, EVP
Exercise	8:30 AM – 11:45 AM	R. Jackson, Facilitator
Executive Briefing	11:45 AM – 12:10 PM	E Chavez, Incident Commander
Press Conference	12:10 PM – 12:30 PM	Communications Team
Break – grab lunch	12:30 PM – 12:45 PM	
Debrief	12:45 PM – 1:20 PM	R. Jackson, Facilitator
Next steps	1:20 PM – 1:30 PM	J. Smith, EVP

Exercise plan
See Chapter 6 for a sample of an Exercise Plan.

Exercise injects
See Chapter 8 for exercise inject samples.

Broadcasts
We find that a video broadcast is much more powerful than a radio broadcast, so EMSS uses them whenever possible. The visual imagery has far more impact – in real time and for memories. Broadcast scripts are written once the overall exercise design has been completed. As the design process moves forward, it is likely that details get changed or interesting nuances are added that will make great media fodder, so we have learned it is best to create the broadcast text last.

Perpetrator video
This is a sample text of a video the "perpetrator" posted on a social media site, such as Twitter, mocking the organization and stating its intention to do harm.

Yo, <<name of the company>>.

Having a bad day? Well frankly, it's only going to worse from here! Notice anything funny??? Who do you think has been filling all your systems with anomalies? Not a coincidence if you think about it. Your security is pathetic!

<<name of the company>> your days are numbered. Go ahead and look, you'll never find us. We're so deep inside your systems your joke of a security department will never even know we're there. And you know what? It wasn't even a challenge to break in. That's the really pathetic part!

Time for us to go, we've got lots of reading to do and info to share... Just think of this as payback for your corporate practices! Toodle-doo, suckers!

News video

This is sample text of a news video that gets shown after the perpetrator has leaked the breach to social media. EMSS usually picks a local news station as the "broadcaster."

> We have just watched a video released on Twitter by someone who claims to have hacked deep into the computer systems of <<company name>>, a <<describe your business such as a "software company">> located here in <<your city name>>. The alleged perpetrator is threatening to release critical customer information and sensitive company information.
>
> <drop in snippets of the rant>>
>
> We have a team en route to <<company name>> to find out more information. Reporting on a breaking news story of an alleged hack at <<company name>>, this is <<reporter name>>. We'll keep you posted as the story develops.

Phone directory

SIMULATION TEAM PHONE DIRECTORY

Exercise simulation team – they create the world for you!

When calling the Simulation Team, please remember:

1. The Genius-of-all-trades can be anyone you want them to be.
2. They will answer the phone with "May I help you?" You then tell them who you are looking for, I.E. Police, FBI, Homeland Security. etc. and they turn into that entity.
3. If you need to find out "real information" (a fact) from a <<company name>> person or department, you may call them directly – tell them you are in an company emergency exercise (without the details) and need information to answer a question or resolve a problem.
4. The Simulation team has limited phones – if you call a number and get voice mail, don't leave a message. Just wait a few minutes and call back or try another Sim Team member. If it is busy, try again in a few minutes...just like real life.

City Government, any department or person	X1234	Office supply vendor	X7890
Contractor, any	X2345	Phone service – Cell, any vendor	X1234
Executive, any	X3456	Police Department	X1234
FBI	x1234	Social media, Twitter, FaceBook	X2345
Financial Institution, any	X4567		
Fire Department, any	X5678	Software companies or products, any	X4567
Genius-of-all-trades	X6789		
Genius-of-all-trades	X7890	Structural Engineering firms, any	X5678
Genius-of-all-trades	X1234		
Genius-of-all-trades	X2345	Technology vendors, hardware, any	X6789
Genius-of-all-trades	X3456		
Genius-of-all-trades	X4567	Telecommunications hardware vendor, any	X6598
Hazardous Materials Team	X5678	Telephone: Local carrier	X1234
Hot site vendor (or CoLo site)	X6789	Telephone: Long distance, MCI, ATT, Sprint	X2345
Hotels, any	X7890		
Insurance, any	X1234	Transportation vendors, i.e. buses, shuttles, cabs	X3456
Media, any print	X2345		
Media, any traditional - TV, radio	X5678	Utilities, any others not mentioned in directory	X6789

Participant evaluation

PARTICIPANT EVALUATION FORM

Please circle one response
Strongly Disagree — Neutral — Strongly Agree

Exercise Design

#	Statement	SD		N		SA
1	The exercise scenario was realistic.	1	2	3	4	5
2	The exercise injects were plausible	1	2	3	4	5
3	The exercise length was appropriate.	1	2	3	4	5
4	The exercise encouraged "hands-on" participation.	1	2	3	4	5
5	The scenario was a plausible, "real-world" incident.	1	2	3	4	5

Exercise Experience

#	Statement	SD		N		SA
6	Having everyone in the same room was useful.	1	2	3	4	5
7	The facilitator was effective.	1	2	3	4	5
8	The exercise was a good use of my time.	1	2	3	4	5
9	The exercise was educational.	1	2	3	4	5
10	The exercise was well organized.	1	2	3	4	5
11	The exercise opened my eyes to what a cyber attack could be like.	1	2	3	4	5
12	The exercise met my expectations.	1	2	3	4	5

Company Planning and Approach

#	Statement	SD		N		SA
13	Management supports the business continuity effort at here.	1	2	3	4	5
14	I feel I have been given the right amount of training to be effective in responding to a cyber attack.	1	2	3	4	5
15	We should do these exercises more often.	1	2	3	4	5
16	I feel prepared to respond to a cyber attack here.	1	2	3	4	5

Department Planning and Approach

#	Statement	SD		N		SA
17	It would be helpful if others in my dept./business unit could participate in an exercise like this.	1	2	3	4	5
18	Our team is adequately prepared to respond to a cyber attack.	1	2	3	4	5
19	Our plan for responding to a cyber attack is complete.	1	2	3	4	5
20	If you have any other observations or suggestions you would like to share, please note them below.					

Simulation Team exercise evaluation

SIMULATION TEAM EXERCISE EVALUATION FORM

Thank you for participating in this exercise! Your feedback is very important to to making future exercises as effective as possible. Please take a few moments to comment on your experience.

1. Overall, what did you think of the exercise?

2. How was your experience as a Sim Team member? Please explain.

3. What did you think was the most helpful?

4. What could we improve on?

5. How could we make the Sim Team experience better?

6. Is there anything in particular that you would like to see in future exercises?

It takes as much energy to wish as it does to plan.
— ***Eleanor Roosevelt***

Evaluator / Observer form

EVALUATOR / OBSERVER FORM
Observer name: Team observing:
Role of the Evaluator/Observer The exercise Design Team has developed these objectives with a series of metrics for the exercise. The evaluators will use the metrics to determine if the objectives have been met. We understand that this will be somewhat subjective by the evaluator and you can't be everywhere at once. Just do the best you can. The following methods may be used: ▶ Observe participants. ▶ Look at situation boards and reporting forms. ▶ Check any reports. ▶ Talk with participants. ▶ Be a "fly on the wall" — listen in on conversations and informal briefings. ▶ Look for 'teachable moments.'
Exercise objectives List all of the exercise objectives here.
Exercise Metrics The above objectives will be evaluated on feedback using three methodologies: the debrief sessions, written evaluations, and observations by the observer and facilitator. Please return your written comments to exercise facilitator at the end of the day.
Please list three things the team you were observing did well: 1 2. 3.
Please list three things the team did that need improvement: 1. 2. 3.

Executive briefing document

EXECUTIVE BRIEFING DOCUMENT

Section 1: Your role as executive in this exercise
- ▶ Your task is to play your "usual executive role" by asking pertinent questions on how this situation is impacting departments, regions, and the ability of team to continue to operate the business.
- ▶ We ask that you stay in role, and play this situation as if it were *really* happening. You are there to receive a briefing on the current status of this significant and on-going event.
- ▶ Call into the Executive Emergency conference bridge line at the designated time and the Incident Commander will greet you and conduct an update briefing with your team.

Please remember that the team will have been working through this exercise scenario since <<*note the time the exercise began*>>.

Note: If this were a real on-going event, this would not be your first briefing. In a real event you would, of course, have had several briefings prior to this call.

Section 2: The narrative
Include the exercise artificialities, assumptions and narrative here.

Section 3: Key Issues
Include any key issues here that you think the executives will want to focus on. This is a bit of insurance in case they didn't have time to read and digest the narrative. You want them to be in role and, especially, to be successful.
Inability to transact business

- ▶ Potential release of sensitive company and customer information
- ▶ Reputational impact
- ▶ Extensive media coverage of event
- ▶ Potential decrease in stock price

*The only difference between a mob
and a trained army is organization.*
— *Calvin Coolidge*

Summary

One of the most critical aspects in exercise design is to stay organized and on schedule. A clear path to success is a well-thought-out project plan and a clear idea of all of the documents and audio-visual tools that you will need to create. Spend time at the beginning of the process to get organized, and then stay on track through to exercise day.

Printed in Great Britain
by Amazon